PHANTOM FELINES
and Other Ghostly Animals

D1506270

OTHER BOOKS BY GERINA DUNWICH

Candlelight Spells

Wicca Candle Magick

Circle of Shadows

The Concise Lexicon of the Occult

Wicca Craft

Wicca Love Spells

The Wicca Spellbook

The Wicca Book of Days

The Wicca Source Book

The Wicca Garden

A Wiccan's Guide to Prophecy & Divination

Everyday Wicca

Magick Potions

Wicca A to Z

The Pagan Book of Halloween

Your Magickal Cat

The Modern Witch's Complete Sourcebook

Exploring Spellcraft

Herbal Magick

The Cauldron of Dreams

A Witch's Guide to Ghosts and the Supernatural

Dunwich's Guide to Gemstone Sorcery

PHANTOM FELINES

and Other Ghostly Animals

GERINA DUNWICH

CITADEL PRESS
Kensington Publishing Corp.
www.kensingtonbooks.com

CITADEL PRESS BOOKS are published by

Kensington Publishing Corp.
850 Third Avenue
New York, NY 10022

All Kensington titles, imprints, and distributed lines are available at special quantity discounts for bulk purchases for sales promotions, premiums, fund-raising, educational, or institutional use. Special book excerpts or customized printings can also be created to fit specific needs. For details, write or phone the office of the Kensington special sales manager: Kensington Publishing Corp., 850 Third Avenue, New York, NY 10022, attn: Special Sales Department; phone 1-800-221-2647.

CITADEL PRESS and the Citadel logo are Reg. U.S. Pat. & TM Off.

First printing: September 2006

10 9 8 7 6 5 4 3 2 1

Printed in the United States of America

Library of Congress Control Number: 2006926714

ISBN 0-8065-2752-8

CONTENTS

Contents

Contents

3. Hounds and Hauntings 83

Contents

INTRODUCTION

My fascination with ghosts and hauntings, along with a serious interest in witchcraft and most things of an occult nature, began as a child growing up in the Midwest. My first encounters with the paranormal all took place at my grandmother's house in Riverside, Illinois, which I (and other members of my family) truly believe was haunted by the spirit of my grandfather who died there. I felt something invisible was watching me whenever I was in that house, and while exploring the attic there once, a misty form materialized out of the shadows and chased me down the attic stairs. It frightened me at the time, but also increased my curiosity in that type of phenomena.

I became interested in animal ghosts after living in an old house in New York that was frequently visited by a supernatural bat. There I also witnessed a phantom feline (the so-called Devil Cat of Fort Covington) with my very own eyes. These unique experiences helped perk my interest in professional ghost hunting and eventually led me to form the Paranormal Animal Research Group, which investigates animal-related hauntings and studies animal sensitivity to paranormal anomalies.

As an investigator of the paranormal, I've had the opportunity to meet and talk with numerous people from around the world who've also had encounters with otherworldly animals. Most of their experiences involve the spirits of deceased pets. However, experiences with phantom livestock, wild animals, and even animal spirit guides have been reported as well.

A number of these individuals have graciously allowed me to include their personal stories in this book. Some are guaranteed to give you goose bumps, some will warm your heart, and some are sure to bring tears to your eyes. But the one common thread that links these stories together is the amazing fact that they're all true! I hope you will enjoy reading them as much as I have.

And if by chance you should feel something invisible brush against your legs, lick your hand, or move across your bed in the middle of the night, do not be alarmed. It might just be a phantom feline, a haunting hound, or some other ghostly animal visiting you from beyond the grave.

ACKNOWLEDGMENTS

I would like to give thanks to all the individuals who contributed stories about animal ghosts. Without you this book could not have been possible. And a very special "thank-you" to Al for all of the support and inspiration you've given me.

1

UNDERSTANDING PARANORMAL ANIMALS

"Never dismiss the possibility of the existence of apparitions for not only does this attitude resemble that of the proverbial ostrich, but it could result in some unpleasant experiences if you come face to face with a ghost." —Andrew Green, parapsychologist.

Throughout the centuries, tales exist of animal apparitions appearing to the living as a warning of impending danger or death. Animal spirits have also been known to appear, either visually or in dreams, to act as guides or to comfort people in their grief over the death of a beloved pet. There are even terrifying stories about animals returning from the dead to seek revenge against their tormentors and killers. But the main reasons why most animal ghosts (particularly those of pets) appear to the living are to let their loved ones know they are all right in the next world, or simply to bid them farewell. This type of paranormal phenomena most frequently occurs when there exists a strong emotional bond between individuals and their pets.

Often, after the animal's "mission" has been accomplished, its spirit finds peace and is never seen or heard again. (That is, of course, until the animal and its loved ones are reunited on the other side.)

Haunted Places

Just as there are houses and other areas that are haunted by the ghosts of persons who died or were killed there, so, too, are there many places where the ghosts of cats, dogs, birds, and other animals have been encountered. The Whaley House and Arundel Castle are two such places.

Preserved as a historic museum, the Whaley House in San Diego is officially recognized as "a genuine haunted house" by both the United States Chamber of Commerce and the State of California. Within this mid-nineteenth-century mansion, visitors have sighted the fleeting apparition of a dog on a number of occasions. On the other side of the Atlantic, a spectral white bird is but one of the many ghosts that haunt England's eleventh-century Arundel Castle. When a death is imminent, the bird appears and flutters against the windows.

Another interesting place where animal ghosts have been sighted is the L.A. Pet Memorial Park (originally called L.A. Pet Cemetery), which is located in Calabasas, California. Founded and dedicated on September 4, 1928, it is the oldest facility of its kind on the West Coast. Its beautifully landscaped hillsides are the final resting place for many of Hollywood's animal actors (such as Hopalong Cassidy's horse, Topper, and the Little Rascals' pit bull, Petey) as well as the pets of movie stars and the rich and famous. Over 40,000 animals, ranging from hamsters to lions, are interred there. However, the majority of the graves belong to dogs and cats.

Many different animal ghosts have been sighted at L.A. Pet Memorial Park over the years. But the one that draws the most attention is Kabar—a Great Dane whose master was the Italian film star and heartthrob, Rudolph Valentino. The dog, which died in 1929 (three years after Valentino's death) is said to be a friendly and playful ghost that appears from time to time and licks the people who walk by his grave. Some visitors to the cemetery have also reported hearing the sound of a dog panting in the area where the Great Dane is buried.

My husband and I visited the pet cemetery on Halloween of 2005. We arrived there at 9:30 a.m. and walked around the grounds and took pictures. We also took a number of electromagnetic field readings with our ELF-Zone detector, all of which were in the normal range. (A high or fluctuating reading is, in some cases, an indicator of paranormal activity.) After an hour and a half, we finally located the grave of Kabar and took another reading; it was normal. I then knelt down, placed the palms of my hands upon Kabar's grave marker, and started talking to the dog as if he were still alive. Neither my husband nor I felt any presence or cold spots, and Kabar gave us no sign. (Perhaps it was because his spirit was no longer earthbound, or maybe he somehow sensed I was a "cat person" at heart.)

After a while we moved on and came upon the grave marker of Hopalong Cassidy's horse, Topper. We said hello to him, took another reading, and then decided to call it a day. As we walked away from the grave, both my husband and I heard the clear and distinct whinny of a horse. It was quite an odd thing since there were no horses (at least not living ones) anywhere around and, with the exception of a gardener who was working on the other side of the cemetery, we were the only ones there. We left the cemetery with the feeling that Topper's ghost had acknowledged our presence.

Earthbound Spirits and Spectral Sightings

Not all animals that die return as ghosts or spirits. The reason for this can be attributed to several factors. Just as a violent or tragic death can prevent many a human spirit from resting in peace, so, too, can a death of this type cause an animal spirit to remain earthbound. In addition, a strong emotional bond between a human and an animal or a person's constant grieving for the loss of a beloved pet can sometimes serve as a catalyst for the animal's ghostly departure from the grave. In such cases, however, the spirit usually remains earthbound for only a brief time.

Some people believe that only intelligent species possess spirits (or souls). But I personally believe that all living creatures do. Hauntings involving many different types of animals have been reported throughout the centuries and in just about every part of the world. But judging by the types of animals reported in ghost sightings, it appears to be far more common for the spirits of cats, dogs, and horses to haunt the areas where their deaths occurred or to attempt contact with the living.

Spectral sightings are a universal phenomenon and ghost stories of all types can be found in every culture throughout the world. However, Great Britain, with all of its ancient castles, graveyards, and battle sites, seems to rank as the most haunted place on earth. In her book, *500 British Ghosts and Hauntings*, Sarah Hapgood says, "Great Britain has more ghosts per square mile than any other country in the world." This fact, according to Hapgood, is a source of pride for many Britons.

Animal Sensitivity to Hauntings

Many believe that animals, including pets, are gifted with a higher degree of psychic sensitivity than the average person. They possess the uncanny ability to sense impending danger and, where the supernatural is concerned, quite often are able to see, hear, and feel things that normal human senses are unable to perceive.

In *Harper's Encyclopedia of Mystical and Paranormal Experience*, Rosemary Ellen Guiley states, "Many psychics like to have animals accompany them when they are investigating apparitions and haunted houses, because animals are assumed to be more sensitive to ghosts and spirits." She also says, "Many dogs and cats have been known to visibly react with fear when placed in a suspected haunted house," which I know to be a fact from my own personal experiences.

Many years ago my family lived in an old Victorian house in upstate New York. The place was haunted, and strange, unexplained things happened there from time to time, such as loud banging sounds coming from the attic, window shades rolling up by themselves, and grayish misty forms that materialized from out of nowhere, glide across a room, and then suddenly vanish. Prior to such happenings, one of our housecats—a female Himalayan named Delilah—would often exhibit signs of uneasiness and go into hiding. Occasionally she stalked or stared at something that was invisible to our eyes. The fur on her back and tail would bristle all of a sudden, she'd hiss or give a low growl, and then take off running as though frightened by something that only she could see. This curious behavior was almost always observed in the evening hours and was usually accompanied by a noticeable drop in the room's temperature—a phenomenon commonly associated with ghostly visitations.

Animal Hauntings vs. Human Hauntings

As a paranormal investigator who specializes in animal apparitions and hauntings, two of the questions I'm frequently asked are: What are the symptoms of an animal haunting (as opposed to a human haunting) and how can you determine whether an unseen ghost or spirit is one belonging to an animal or a human?

In response to these questions, a typical animal haunting can produce one or more of the following symptoms:

- Cold spots, which indicate the absorption of heat energy by an earthbound spirit, can sometimes be felt at a location where an animal has died or been killed. Many ghost hunters employ infrared thermal scanners to detect cold spots, which can range from twenty-five degrees to sixty degrees colder than the surrounding air temperature. This type of phenomena is also experienced in buildings and places haunted by human ghosts.

- Animal sounds, such as meowing, barking, growling, hissing, chirping, scratching, and the fluttering of wings, or the pitter-patter of paws when no animals are present. It is also possible for these types of sounds to be picked up on magnetic recording tapes. Typically, EVP (electronic voice phenomenon) animal sounds are inaudible during recording but are heard when the tape is played back.

- The sounds of things crashing to the floor or shattering are common in hauntings. Almost always, upon investigation, nothing in the house is found to have been disturbed.

- Doors that are pushed open on their own can indicate the presence of an animal ghost or spirit, although this phenomenon frequently occurs in human hauntings as well. However, if the turning of doorknobs or the closing of doors is observed, this almost always indicates a human, and not an animal, haunting. (Unless, of course, the animal possessed in life a rare, but not unheard of, talent for turning knobs or closing doors.)

- The unexplained disappearance of small items and their equally inexplicable reappearance, often in unusual locations. Although this type of phenomena can also occur in human hauntings, it is often attributed to phantom cats and dogs, especially if the animal, during its life, had the habit of making off with small objects and hiding them.

- The physical sensation of an animal pawing, licking, or nipping your skin; rubbing against your leg; running or flying past you; jumping up on the bed; and so forth. Other sensations can include the feeling of being followed or watched when no one else is around.

- The appearance of orbs with long contrails can be an indication of paranormal activity. Appearing as round or diffuse luminaries that defy gravity and rapidly change direction, orbs are believed by many paranormal researchers to be a form of energy of unknown origin. These anomalies are not normally visible to the naked eye, although ghost lights (which are similar to orbs in their shape in behavior) are. Orbs can, however, be viewed through infrared monitors and even captured on photographic film. (It is rare to capture a true ghost orb on film, and, despite the claims of many amateur ghost hunters, the majority of "orbs" appearing in pictures taken by modern digital cameras are nothing more than airborne dust particles reflecting the light from the flash. Rain droplets, snow, pollen, flying insects, and other things not of a paranormal origin can also be mistaken as ghost orbs.)

🐾 Smells—either pleasant or unpleasant—that are associated with animals are common. This can include the distinctive odor of pet food, excrement, catnip, a leather collar, or even a rubber chew toy.

🐾 Lights and electrical appliances are often affected by ghosts of both the animal and human variety, and it is not uncommon for them to turn on and off by themselves and, in some cases, even short out. The reason for this, many paranormal researchers believe, is because ghosts are made up of electromagnetic and electrostatic energy.

🐾 Visible apparitions are probably the less common of all the haunting symptoms. But when they do manifest, they may appear to the eyewitness as being real and corporeal with definable form and features. Or they may instead take on a luminous, transparent, or wispy appearance. Apparitions have been observed moving through walls, closed doors, and solid objects. And contrary to popular belief, they can also cast shadows and be reflected in mirrors. It seems to be the nature of most apparitions to appear and disappear suddenly, while some just fade away as though evaporating into the ethers. In addition to apparitions, shadows in animal shapes have also been observed and are usually seen out of the corner of one's eye.

There are also a number of signs that definitely point to a haunting that is human, and not animal, in nature. These include the following:

🐾 The materialization of human apparitions and human-shaped shadows and shapes.

🐾 The sound of a disembodied human voice whispering, crying, singing, laughing, calling one's name, etc. The sound of ghostly music and human footsteps are also sometimes heard.

🐾 The smell of perfume, cologne, or after-shave lotion.

🐾 Objects that are thrown across the room or the moving around of furniture by unseen forces.

Sometimes animal and human ghosts or spirits will coexist within a particular dwelling or location. When this happens, symptoms of either, or both, types of hauntings may be experienced. The apparition of a horse-drawn carriage and its coachman is but one example of a paranormal animal/human coexistence.

There are, of course, times when it is difficult or even impossible for one (including a well-seasoned ghost hunter) to determine whether a ghost or spirit is of animal or human origin. For example, if it is unknown who or what died in a particular house and a person there merely senses that he or she is being watched when alone or hears the sound of a creaking door, it would be next to impossible to know with any amount of certainty if an animal or human spirit was at work. In such cases, the services of a reputable psychic or spiritualist medium can sometimes prove to be beneficial.

It is not uncommon for some paranormal researchers to work side by side with psychics. However, many prefer to take a strictly scientific approach when investigating ghostly phenomena and anomalies.

Communicating with Four-Legged Ghosts

Some ghosts of animals and humans are thought to be earthbound spirits of the dead. These entities are able to interact with the living and possess an intelligence that opens the door to communication on a mediumistic level.

Communication between living humans and the earthbound spirits of animals is not impossible, although it does have its limitations. As with living animals, those in spirit form may understand certain spoken words and commands, as well as the tone of a human voice. Depending on the type of animal, they may respond to the sound of their name. To make their presence known or, as in some cases, to warn the living of impending danger, they sometimes emit a ghostly barking, growling, purring, hissing, wailing, or whimpering. In the case of ghost birds, the sound of chirping or the fluttering of invisible wings may be heard.

Sometimes such entities communicate with humans simply by leaving them with the feeling of being brushed against, pawed, or sometimes even licked or nibbled. A misty animal apparition that appears for a second or two and then vanishes from sight can be a ghost animal's subtle way of communicating to the living that it is still around, missing its human or animal companions, or perhaps watching over the household from the other side.

Communication with animal ghosts must be approached differently than communication with the ghosts of human beings. Obviously such devices and methods as Ouija boards and automatic writing are not very effective when it comes to dealing with spirits that are incapable of reading or writing.

I have found that the best way of making contact is to go to an area where the animal died or has been frequently sighted, move very slowly as to not frighten it away, and talk to it in the same manner as you would a living animal. Call out its name and make kissing sounds or whistle, if that is the sort of thing it responded to in life. When you begin to sense the animal's presence, a simple "here, boy" or "kitty, kitty" will probably work better for you than asking your dearly departed Rover or Fluffy what it's like in the afterworld or asking them to forgive you for having to put them to sleep. Do not expect them to understand questions or everything you say. Remember, you are talking to an animal after all. It does not speak in a human tongue.

If you sense that the spirit is afraid, agitated, or in pain, the best thing to do is speak to it in a soothing and comforting tone. (This approach also works well with human spirits.) However, instructing them to "go into the light" will most likely yield the same results as talking to the wall in Pig Latin.

I must add, however, that I have heard a handful of allegedly true stories about ghost animals speaking to the living in human voice—either audibly or telepathically. But such cases appear to be extremely rare, and none, to the best of my knowledge, have ever been officially documented. Of course that's not to rule out that such things are completely out of the realm of possibility.

It is believed among many paranormal investigators that ghosts (being a form of energy) and paranormal activity are greatly influenced by solar storms and the earth's geomagnetic fields.

A solar storm occurs when the sun creates solar flares that send charged particles to the earth. These particles cause a magnetic shift, which increases the planet's geomagnetic fields. Researchers around the world have discovered that paranormal activity greatly increases in strength and clarity during this time and they attribute this to the excess energy in the air acting as a kind of mega power supply for spirits, which are known to feed off electrical sources such as batteries and electrical appliances. Solar storms also seem to create an atmospheric condition conducive to spirit contact and communication.

To access the National Oceanic and Atmospheric Administration (NOAA) online Solar X-Ray and Geomagnetic Field Monitors, please go to the following website: www.n3kl.org/sun/status.html.

Paranormal activity can also be very active during the times of the full moon and the new moon, as these lunar phases are known to generate peak magnetic fields. Throughout history, the nights of the vernal and autumnal equinoxes and the summer and winter solstices have been believed by many people to also be times when activity of a paranormal nature is higher than normal. But according to most modern-day witches and pagans, the most favorable (and festive) time of the year during which to encounter spirits and communicate with the dead is All Hallows' Eve (popularly known as Halloween).

Starting at sundown on October 31, the invisible "veil" between the worlds of the living and the dead is said to be at its thinnest point in the year, allowing the spirits of animals and humans to pass through into our world and roam the earth until the setting of the sun on November 1. This belief originated with the ancient Celts, whose festival of the dead, *Samhain* (pronounced "sow-an"), was observed each year at this time. (It is interesting to note that the ancient Celts also believed that on this most sacred of nights, the souls of condemned humans were sentenced by the Lord of the Dead to spend one entire year in the afterlife in the form of an animal.)

Residual Hauntings

Ghosts that do not respond to attempts at communication and repeat their actions over and over similar to a loop of movie film are considered by many paranormal experts to be not earthbound spirits, but rather some sort of psychic recording of a past event that has imprinted itself on the environment.

Hauntings of this nature are commonly referred to as "residual hauntings" or "recordings," and one good example of such would be an apparition of a horse drawn carriage that appears at the same location and same time every year on the anniversary date of a fatal accident.

Residual hauntings can involve the apparitions of animals, people, and even inanimate objects such as ships and automobiles.

Some residual hauntings cease after a period of time, whereas others have been known to persist for hundreds of years. Why some continue on longer than others is not known. And what it is exactly that creates these phenomena is not, at the present time, completely understood.

An Interview with Jeff Belanger

Jeff Belanger, who launched the popular Ghostvillage.com website on Halloween of 1999, first experienced ghosts and the supernatural at the age of ten. He has been writing about these subjects since 1997 when he conducted an interview with the famed husband-and-wife ghost-hunting team of Ed and Lorraine Warren. Belanger has written on the topic of the supernatural for many magazines, and is the author of the following books: *The World's Most Haunted Places: From the Secret Files of Ghostvillage. com* (New Page Books, 2004), *Communicating with the Dead: Reach Beyond the Grave* (New Page Books, 2005), and *The Encyclopedia of Haunted Places: Ghostly Locales from Around the World* (New Page Books, 2005). He is a graduate of Hofstra University and a member of the American Society of Psychical Research. His website is www.GhostVillage.com.

I had the pleasure of interviewing Jeff Belanger in September of 2005. I posed the following twelve questions to him about animal ghosts and hauntings, which are followed by his straightforward replies:

Q: How did you first become interested in the subject of ghosts?

A: I grew up in a very historic and haunted old New England town where it wasn't uncommon to see houses that were two hundred or more years old. At age ten, I had more than one friend who claimed their old home was haunted. We would have sleepovers and break out the Ouija board—and then we would search the house for the things that bumped and creaked in the night. I found the descriptions of my friends' ghost encounters so compelling that I've been hooked ever since.

Q: Have you personally ever seen, felt, heard, or sensed an animal ghost?

A: I'm not sure. In the house I grew up in, everyone in my family had heard something walking in the front hallway. I recall one afternoon as a teenager being home alone. I walked through the front hallway and looked down at a miniature chair my mother had along the wall, and just as it caught my attention, the chair slid out from the wall about six inches—as if something had bumped into it. I honestly can't say what that something may have been, but it certainly wasn't me.

Q: Why do some animal spirits remain earthbound after the death of the physical body while others apparently do not?

A: Some animal ghosts are simply psychic impressions left in an area—like a movie that plays over and over again, and some people can tune in to that movie under certain circumstances. It doesn't mean the animal is still there and can interact with us—just that it was there at one time and we perceive it as an animal ghost. I imagine some animal spirits remain earthbound for the same reasons that some humans do—they don't realize that they're dead or they have something they feel obligated to do before they can move on (maybe keep a protective eye on their owner or claw at the couch one last time).

Q: There are many reports of houses, castles, and other dwellings being haunted by cats, dogs, and even phantom horse-drawn carriages. What causes ghosts to haunt certain places?

A: It seems that spirits of all kinds tend to stick around where they were most comfortable, and that's usually home. In some cases, these animal spirits may be running through the routines they ran through in life, or they may feel the need to keep a watchful eye on the location they loved.

Q: If a person witnesses the apparition of an animal (or any other type of ghost, for that matter), how can he or she be certain that the apparition is actually a ghost and not a hallucination or a trick of the eyes?

A: Ghost encounters of all kinds are completely personal and subjective experiences, and truth is absolutely relative. Some people are so eager to believe in spirit contact that they seek (and usually find) signs everywhere. Others are more skeptical and won't believe until the spirit of someone they knew in life taps them on their shoulder. No one can tell another what's the real experience and what's a trick of the eye. It comes down to the individual who has the encounter and what they perceive it to be. One person's darting shadow is another person's ghost.

Q: In cases of non-apparitional hauntings, are there any ways for a person to determine whether a ghost is that of a human or an animal?

A: You have to look for characteristic patterns. Animals wouldn't typically open and close the head-level kitchen cabinets, and humans don't typically brush up against other people's ankles. Individual perception is everything when it comes to ghosts—it's a gut feeling (or maybe even a sixth sense, if you will) that helps the living witness determine exactly who or what may be haunting them.

Q: Some people have reported hearing their deceased pets. Can EVP (electronic voice phenomenon) recordings pick up paranormal animal sounds (such as meowing, barking, or chirping) in the same way it does human voices? Are you familiar with any such cases?

A: I have heard a lot of EVP recordings that have many strange sounds in them, some that one might interpret to be non-human sounds. Though I haven't personally heard a distinctly animal EVP, I don't see why it wouldn't be possible.

Q: Various methods, ranging from Ouija boards to séances, have been employed for communication with the spirits of dead people. Do you believe it is also possible to communicate with the spirits of animals, and if so, how would one go about making contact with, let's say, the spirit of a deceased family pet?

A: For any kind of communication to occur, there needs to be at least two willing parties involved—this is also true in the world of the living. If I walk into my backyard and yell, "Hello," and no one is there to hear it, then I'm not communicating. I have a pet parakeet named Mambo who flies around my house all day and often sits on my shoulder while I'm working. Though I don't speak bird (and he doesn't speak human), I believe we communicate—I can tell from his body language and peeps when he's feeling playful or when he's feeling mellow. Without being able to physically see or hear him, I don't know how we would communicate. A Ouija board would likely mean the same thing to Mambo in death as it does in life—to him it may look a little like the newspaper he so often poops on in his cage. That's not to say that I may not hear the phantom flutter of his wings one day letting me know that he's still around. But I don't know how I could communicate with him in death. All that being said, I have met animal healers and psychics who claim to be able to communicate with animals in both life and death, but I don't feel I personally have this gift.

Q: Many people are afraid of ghosts. As a ghost investigator, do you feel such fears are unfounded?

A: A lot of us fear what we don't understand. For many people, ghost experiences aren't something they're allowed to talk about. So if it happens to someone, they're afraid of many things— their own mortality, if they're sane, and concern that they may have to bear the burden of having this experience and not being able to talk about it with anyone for fear of ridicule. I'm glad to say I've seen this changing. People are discussing the subject more, books like this one talk about the experience, many websites have forums for people to share their own encounters, and ghosts have even gone mainstream on TV and in movies. It's important we keep talking about them.

Q: Is there a difference between the spirit and the soul?

A: It depends on your belief system, but many faiths use these words interchangeably. For me, I don't think it matters what terminology you use, so long as you acknowledge that "thing" inside of you and inside of every other living thing that makes us something more than creatures that just eat, sleep, procreate, and repeat.

Q: Some people do not believe that animals have souls. Others believe that only human beings have individual souls and that every animal is part of the "group soul" of its species. Do you have any thoughts on this?

A: One of the experiences I had as a child that convinced me there must be something after death was witnessing my grandfather's body at his wake. It was clearly my grandfather's body, but it didn't really look like him—that "thing" inside of him that made him who he was, was gone. If we all had no soul or spirit, then he should have looked like he was sleeping, but he didn't. I've witnessed the same phenomena with my pets over the years—that life force and personality, which made the animal something more than just an object, left after they died. I can only give my own opinion here as some would consider the idea heresy, but I believe all living things move on to something else—to what or where, I don't know. Maybe some day I'll come back and tell you.

Q: Your GhostVillage website features a large number of true ghost stories. Can you talk about some of the most interesting or unusual animal-related ones that you've received?

A: We've published more than a couple ghost encounters from people who believe their pets have visited them. Some people wrote that they felt something invisible pounce on their bed beside them, they watched little paw prints push into the bedspread just as their cat used to do and then the footprints stopped and the event was over. I once spoke to a family of four who all witnessed the shadow of what appeared to be their deceased dog dart through the room. And several witnesses have claimed to feel a cat brush against their legs though their cat passed away in some cases months earlier. Most people who have these pet encounters don't seem frightened because the presence is somehow familiar. Once the encounter ends, most claim the experience was actually very special and comforting to know their pets are still around and are making themselves known.

2

PHANTOM FELINES

The Devil Cat of Fort Covington

by Gerina Dunwich

F ort Covington, located in northern New York State, is a rural community made up of many turn-of-the-century homes, farms, and woodlands. It borders the Akwasasne Indian Reservation, and parts of the town are said to have been built over old Indian burial ground. Like many small communities throughout America, Fort Covington (or simply "The Fort" as the locals call it) has its share of local legends—the infamous Devil Cat being one of them.

I first heard about the Devil Cat shortly after moving to Fort Covington in December of 1993. One neighbor described the creature as a "hellish" cat with eerie glowing eyes and fur as black as pitch. It reportedly possessed a mean disposition and, being supernatural, could not be destroyed by any means. Several people claimed to have shot it dead, only to observe it come back to life and take off running.

Being the cat lover that I am, I found the legend of the Devil Cat to be a rather intriguing one, although the idea of anyone shooting at a cat (even one that was supposedly immune to bullets) did not set well with me. But also being a skeptic by nature, I took it all with a grain of salt. That is until one snowy spring day when I encountered a strange black cat prowling near the barn where one of our cats was nursing her kittens.

It was much larger than any cat I had ever seen before and its fur was matted and riddled with a number of bald patches. Its face was disfigured and utterly grotesque. From the looks of it, the animal appeared to have been in one hell of a catfight. I didn't know if it would try to harm my cat or her kittens, so I attempted to chase it away by rushing toward it while clapping my hands and shouting, "Scat!"

Any normal cat would have taken off like a shot, but this was no ordinary cat. It brazenly turned to face me, arched its back, and began growling like a dog. I stopped dead in my tracks, stunned by the animal's unusual reaction and even feeling a bit apprehensive. After about five seconds, the cat took off and disappeared into the woods behind the barn. Oddly, it left behind no paw prints in the soft, freshly fallen snow, and that's when I realized that I had come face to face with the Devil Cat of Fort Covington.

The Purring

by Brandy Hoffstedder

When I was in my sophomore year of high school, my family and I moved into a large old house on the west side of Binghamton, New York. Built in the late 1800s in the Queen Anne style and gated all around by an ornate fence of rusted wrought iron, it was a house filled with many dark secrets and restless spirits.

One of the invisible occupants of the house was a woman who had lived there in the 1930s and had taken her own life shortly after the death of her only child. Another was an elderly man who died in his sleep in the bedroom I named the Rose Room because of the design of rose bouquets on the room's faded wallpaper.

Strange happenings took place in the house, occurring mainly during the evening hours and experienced by all members of my family. These consisted of lights being turned on and off, the sound of footsteps on the stairs, and mysterious tapping on the stained glass window at the end of the upstairs hall. There was a definite cold spot in one corner of the Rose Room, and even if the furnace was running and the rest of the room was warm and cozy, that corner still felt like the inside of a refrigerator. Sometimes things like keys, books, and saltshakers disappeared for a while and then turned up later in the same spot where last seen, as though they had never been moved.

A few times I heard the distinct sound of a woman gently sobbing. It was very faint and came from the kitchen when no one was in the room. I believe it was the spirit of the woman who committed suicide, and even in death she continued to grieve the loss of her child. My mother and sister and even a few of our guests (all females) also heard the crying woman at different times. But for some funny reason, she only allowed other females to hear her cry. My father, brothers, and male guests never heard her.

The ghost of a cat also haunted the house. None of us actually saw it, but we could tell it was a cat because every now and then we heard a purring sound, and we didn't own a cat at the time. The purring would last for a few seconds, sometimes longer, and if you walked over to where it was coming from, it would then seem to come from the other side of the room. After a while, we started affectionately referring to this unseen cat-spirit as Casper, after the cartoon ghost.

Our dog, Molly, sometimes started barking for no apparent reason and chased after something that none of us were able to see. Since dogs' senses are far sharper than ours and they are able to see and hear things that are normally invisible and inaudible to the eyes and ears of most humans, I believe it's possible Molly could have seen or maybe even picked up Casper's scent and was simply following her natural dog-chase-cat instincts.

It has been many years since my parents sold the haunted house in Binghamton and moved away to another city. I drove past the old place on a rainy day about a year ago and could have sworn I saw a big ginger tabby cat peering out at me from the rain-streaked living room window. But when I blinked my eyes it was no longer there. I've wondered ever since if it might have been our Casper revealing himself to me for just an instant.

Solomon

by Christy Johnson

In October of 1997, my beloved Siamese cat, Solomon, passed away from kidney disease. At the time, I also shared my home with a young kitten, an elderly dog, and an iguana.

Solomon had chosen me a year before on a visit to the local Humane Society when he forcefully got my attention by grabbing hold of my leg and pulling me up against the bars of the cage he was in. There was little doubt that this animal was coming home with me despite the fact that I had no intention of adopting a pet at that time.

A month after Solomon's passing, I was preparing to move out of town and was showing the house to prospective renters for the absentee owner. One evening, two young women came to take a look at the house. Inviting them in, I told them to look around while I sat in the kitchen with the dog and kitten. They took their tour of the bedrooms and, upon coming into the kitchen, commented on the "menagerie" of pets I had. Confused by that comment, I told them that the only pets I had were the kitten and dog sitting with me, and the iguana in a large cage.

One of the young women remarked that I must be mistaken because they had seen a Siamese cat curled up, sleeping, on my pillow on the bed. When they had turned on the light in the room, they had both seen the cat clear as day. I told them I only had the one cat and they insisted on going back to the bedroom to show me the Siamese cat they had seen. We went back into the bedroom, turned on the light, and looked around the room but, of course, there was no cat there. Baffled by this and appearing to be slightly embarrassed, they thanked me for my time and left.

Two other times after this incident, Solomon was "seen" sitting in the window. Both times were by people who either did not know that he had passed away or were not even aware that I had a cat fitting the description.

At the time of this writing, I am currently caring for an old dog that, suffering with congestive heart failure, is reaching the end of his days with me. In relating these incidents, I take great comfort in knowing that physical death is not the end of existence and that, even when our beloved animal friends leave this world, they are not far away.

A House Haunted by Cats

by Janice Essex

In August 1953 my mother (who was pregnant with me), father, and four sisters moved into an old thirteen-room house that had quite a history. Built in the 1890s, it had been a boarding house where many odd things had happened, including the murder of a male occupant.

As my family was moving things into one of the upstairs bedrooms, two of my sisters screamed at our mother that a stray cat ran out of the room. Everyone assumed that it had run in unnoticed while they were busy moving things in, and the incident was soon forgotten. However, through the years there were more and more incidents of fleeting glimpses of a cat.

My aunt and uncle from Oregon came to visit, and when they sat at breakfast the first morning, my aunt remarked about our cat that was upstairs all night. My mother just smiled and said it was a nuisance. Another time, during a bad time in my life, I was lying on the bed crying and I felt the cat lie down beside me.

My first husband and I were living with my mother, and one night after we had been in bed for a while he said, "Get that damn Jiggs (our physical pet cat) off my feet!" I looked and told him there was nothing there. He said "Oh, hell." He, too, had got a glimpse of the "spirit" cat a couple of times before.

When my daughter was almost three years old, I was taking her upstairs to give her a bath. I was standing at the bottom of the stairs with her in front of me at my feet. She looked up the stairway and said, "Oh, Mommy, there's the kitty." I thought it was strange, since babies don't understand about spirits and ghosts. She also said it like it wasn't uncommon for her to see "the kitty."

I have tried to justify these happenings by attributing them to something natural or imagination, but I know what I've seen and can't really rationalize what they were.

The old house has since been torn down. I am now remarried and living in another state, but all this is as fresh in my mind as if it happened yesterday.

Smitty

by Michael John Weaver

My ex-wife's grandmother had a calico cat named Smitty that I knew well but had not seen in some time. I learned upon a visit to her house in the mid-1990s that the cat had been ill and died. I knew nothing about the details.

While sleeping on the couch I had a dream of an invisible cat that I could feel/pet and feed (Smitty was often fed treats from the table), but in this case the food would hover in midair and then vanish as she ate it. I awoke feeling the kneading of cat's paws on me.

I shared this experience with my ex-wife and she informed me that Smitty in her final days had indeed stopped eating—even hand-offered human food treats.

As an investigator of paranormal phenomena I realize there are alternative explanations, like my acquiring the information via ESP from my ex-wife or her grandmother and then having the dream. I also realize that sleep paralysis can cause physical sensations like the feeling of something sitting on your chest. But to duplicate the kneading of a deceased cat would be stretching this explanation.

The Watchful Spirit

by Tammy Harsma

Starting at a very young age, around eight or nine, I had a spirit cat that used to visit me at night as I was going to bed. I could very distinctly feel it jump up on my bed, walk across the bed and my feet, and curl up next to my legs. This never frightened me. In fact, I never thought it to be out of the ordinary. I'm not sure which cat this was because my family had many as I was growing up, but I had the impression that it was the spirit of a cat that my friends and I had found in the road just after it had been hit by a car. I just stood there feeling so sad for the cat as my friend got a shovel to remove the poor animal out of the road. It has been about thirty-three years and many homes later, but this cat still visits me occasionally to this day.

I have had other encounters as well, mostly the "catching something out of the corner of your eye" variety, but I had one very unique encounter about three years ago.

In July 2001 I lost a cat that was *very* special to me. I had him for thirteen and a half years, through hard times and good times; he was always there with me. My family and I knew that the day Stinky (yes, Stinky) died was going to be difficult for me. What we hadn't realized was how hard it was going to be on my other cat, Kitten. She was very lonely without him.

Kitten never seemed to rebound from Stinky's death, so I thought the best thing to do would be to bring another cat into the home that she could befriend. My husband and I agreed that we would get a kitten and give it to my daughter as a birthday present.

From the minute Boomer came into our home he just seemed to fit into the family. What a personality! I have to say he reminded me a lot of my beloved Stinky. Within months it seemed as if Boomer had always been with us. One game the little guy developed was to try to run into my bedroom whenever the door was opened. I guess his curiosity got the better of him (as the saying goes) because that door was always closed and no cats were allowed into that room—it was off limits.

One night a few months after Boomer had joined us, I woke very suddenly from my sleep. It wasn't from a bad dream or from a noise; I just opened my eyes. I was facing my husband, whose back was to me. As my eyes adjusted to the darkness I noticed the outline of a cat sitting next to my husband's head. I could see that the cat was staring at my husband, and my first thought was, That darn cat snuck into the bedroom!

Well, as I lay there wondering if I should reach out and grab him or just forget about it and go back to sleep, I could see that he was turning toward me. I closed my eyes; I didn't want him to know I was awake and spook him and have him run under the bed or get him all riled up. A few minutes passed and I opened my eyes—no cat. *Darn! He must have run under the bed.*

I decided that I would make a pit stop to the bathroom and then open the bedroom door and walk to my daughter's bedroom in the hopes that Boomer would follow me. As I walked into my daughter's bedroom I noticed that lying on my daughter's bed were both cats—sleeping.

I wasn't frightened, but I knew that Stinky had come for a visit. I haven't seen him since then, but occasionally the cats look up at the top of the stairs as if something is there. We know that Stinky is watching over our family.

Spirit in the Storm

by Samantha Williams

When I was eighteen years old I lost a cat named Digger ("Diggy" for short). This beautiful "lady of fur and razor blades" was my constant companion for more than seven years. She was also my first partner when it came to working magick of any kind—curling up before the altar, sitting in my lap during tarot and rune readings, blessing the candles by rubbing her face and tail over the wicks. She helped to raise quite a bit of power with her tiger's purr!

When she passed away, nothing seemed to feel right. I would cast circle for ritual and there would be a "dead" spot right in front of the altar stone in my ritual room. I felt that after she passed on, she wasn't hanging around to keep me company. I couldn't sense her anywhere.

One night during a thunderstorm I couldn't sleep. I realized I hadn't said good-bye to Diggy or told her all I needed to. I got up and went into the ritual room and cast circle. I entered, sat down, and had a good long cry. I talked to Diggy and told her how much I missed her and loved her still.

Well, after that good cry I heard her "meow," and I looked up. She sat in front of me, swishing her tail. I felt her step into my lap and lie down and curl her face into her paws and begin to purr. I couldn't touch her but I saw her and felt her. I know that this was her way of telling me not to worry about her, that she was doing well where she was now. In addition, I could tell that she dined on "salmon croquets and cream" whenever she chose.

The storm passed while I sat and held her. And when she had to leave, I let her, knowing she still loved me and missed me, too.

The Orange Cat

by Kimberly Peats

My husband and I lived in an apartment complex with our teacup poodle named Trigger. He was smaller than a cat, so we did not have to pay a $100 per month pet fee. We lived there for about two years, then began building a home.

People moved in and out often, so I was not sure that the bright orange cat I saw being chased by children was homeless. I saw him being tormented the next day by some children and shooed them away from him; he ran from me.

It took a few days of coaxing and tuna for him to trust me enough to allow me to stroke him. He was skinny and dirty, but I loved him immediately. I allowed him to follow me to the apartment, but could not risk letting him in and someone turning us in for an increase in rent. I fixed him up a cardboard box with towels and food and water on the porch so he would have a place to stay until we finished building our house. He stayed near, but when I didn't see him for three days, I began to worry.

I had the windows open and heard his cry. I stepped outside

and found him dragging himself across the lawn and children again throwing rocks at him. Only this time, he could not escape. I chased the kids off yet again and once I saw the shape he was in, I called for my husband.

The cat's legs were merely hanging on by threads and his scalp was barely attached to his head. He was a gruesome sight. We wrapped him in a clean towel and raced to the vet's clinic. He purred contentedly all the way there and all throughout the exam. The vet confirmed our worst fear. The cat had been struck by a car a few days ago and must have crawled all the way home. His legs were broken and would have to be amputated. He would never walk again, and his scalp wound contained larvae that had begun to drill into his skull. Throughout this horrible news, the cat continued to purr and act as though nothing could be better.

Although the vet said he could possibly save two of the cat's limbs, there could be no guarantee of his leading a normal life without brain damage. Furthermore, the cost for this care would be nearly $1,500. My husband and I agreed we could not afford that amount, but we felt we were responsible since he spent three days crawling home to us, enduring agony I could not fathom. It was the idea that he might not live a life full and worthy to a cat that made us choose to have him put to sleep. He had a lot of hugs and kisses, and both my husband and I rode home with a heavy heart. We felt completely guilty; had we only allowed him in the apartment he would not have suffered.

A few days later, I took the garbage out to the dumpster where I heard the cat's distinct meow. I thought to myself, Cat, you're okay! I turned to greet him and realized he was not there. Nothing was there. I figured it was my guilt. I went home and did not mention it to my husband.

Yet another few days later, my husband went outside to use the common barbecue grill, and he heard the cat's meow. He reached to greet him and realized the cat was not with us anymore. Later that night I awoke to a warm, purring spot on the bed. I rolled over to give it a good-night pat and realized we did not have a kitty in our bed!

We have had no more visits from the cat since that night. I think he just wanted to say "thank you" to us for letting him go home finally, where he was wanted and loved, and would see us again someday.

Squish and Rameses

by Samantha Williams

This last July, I lost two cats—one week apart. One was a great grand-kitten and another was a great-great-grand-kitten. All of the cats I have owned during the past five years have been lineage cats. I have always owned one of the next generations.

Squish had been the "baby" for a long time and she knew she was the baby. When Silver (her oldest sister) got pregnant, Squish got so jealous of her. Silver demanded all of my time and attention because the unborn ones were active and driving her nuts! When Silver gave birth to two kittens, Squish sniffed them and decided she didn't like them one bit! Silver, while trying to keep her babies warm during those early days of life, accidentally smothered the first one. Silver came running into the living room and got my attention, and I went to see what was wrong. Silver looked at me as if to say, "You can make it better, can't you?"

After the death of the first one, all of the older cats, including Squish, became a "mom" to the last remaining one, which I named Rameses because of the white kohl lines on his eyes. Squish and Rameses became very close and always together. Whether playing, eating, or sleeping, you never saw one without the other.

My house became assaulted by fleas that drove my furry family and me crazy. We tried exterminators and herbal repellants, but nothing seemed to help. I awoke one morning to find Squish dead. The vet later concluded that flea anemia had been the cause. The efforts the vet had been using to treat the fleas had not been enough to prevent her death.

Exactly seven days later, Rameses took a turn for the worst and I rushed him to the vet. There was nothing that could be done. He died later that night. I buried the two young ones, who were inseparable, side by side.

The next night I had a dream about them. I saw them playing and sleeping together and chasing houseflies (their favorite activity). I awoke and realized I heard crunching coming from the kitchen. I thought for a moment that it must be the other "girls" having a midnight snack, but then I realized that they were all at the vet's for observation just in case something might happen while we continued to de-flea the house. I took a peek around the corner and saw the two gray faces of Rameses and Squish eagerly munching away at a dish of cat food. They looked up and saw me, purred, and then vanished. I now know that the longing Rameses had for Squish was so great that he had to go and be with her.

I still cry when I think about what I saw, but I know that the two cats that couldn't bear to be apart were together once again, and I smile, having that knowledge.

This recent Samhain circle, I made a kitty ancestors' altar to remember all my beloved cats, and I felt every one come by and visit during the Dumb Supper feast we held for them. I have dreamed about Squish and Rameses coming back to me one day. I know that when they do, I will welcome them with open arms.

Jamie

(anonymous)

My story is about a cat that was a part of my life for more than nineteen years. Her name was Jamie. She was a great cat and I loved her dearly. Although she was not overly friendly, Jamie occasionally slept at the foot of my bed between my ankles. She was put to sleep in November of 1997 due to failing health.

I had one visit from her afterward. It was just after Christmas the year she died. I was feeling extremely sad that night; I'd had a huge fight with my boyfriend and generally wasn't happy where I was in life. It was also my first Christmas without Jamie. Granted, I wasn't thinking about her at that moment. I was in bed with the lights off, crying to myself and trying to get to sleep. My door was ajar, although I did not see it move, and I heard the soft patter of Jamie's paws come from the door to my bed. I stopped crying and listened. Then I felt her jump up onto the bed. I felt the bedspread give way to her weight (how this is possible when she is a ghost, I don't know) and she curled up at my feet like she used to do. I couldn't believe it. Then I heard her purring.

I was so glad and in awe; my sadness completely melted way. I said out loud, "Hi Jamie, thank you for coming. I've missed you." I was so tempted to reach out and pet her, but I didn't. I didn't move a muscle because, even though I could not see her, I was afraid she'd disappear. She didn't, though, and stayed there until I fell asleep. And funny enough, she didn't feel cold at all; she felt warm.

It was her last good-bye and I am grateful to have been so lucky to have that happen.

The White Cat Apparition

by Linda J. Adams

I have always believed in human spirits but never realized the possibility of animal hauntings until recently. My ninety-year-old house in Collingswood, New Jersey, is haunted by both humans and animals.

The first incident involving a "phantom feline" happened in the early months of 2002. My girlfriend Angie was visiting for the evening. It was around 10 p.m. when she became startled and announced, "Oh, my God, I just saw a white cat run through your living room!" She said that it suddenly appeared and then just as suddenly disappeared. No noise, just a vision. I myself did not see this cat, as I was in the dining room, but I surely took her word for it, especially because of the intense level of ghostly activity otherwise in the house. I did look around after her sighting, but to no avail.

The second incident occurred in October of 2005. I was alone (except for my young son sleeping upstairs in his bed, and our cat, which is brown and black striped, sleeping upstairs in "her" room) and had fallen asleep in the living room while watching TV. I awoke around 3 a.m. and sat up on my couch. I suddenly saw some movement out of the corner of my eye. I looked down and saw what appeared to be an animal of some sort, about the size of a cat and all white, but all I could see was its back. (I initially assumed it was a cat, except the fur was very coarse like that of a guinea pig or a rat, but it appeared too large to be either of those species.) It made its appearance on the floor, along the bottom of the couch, then disappeared underneath the couch.

I froze for a minute or two, not daring to look further. I finally mustered up the courage to look, then peered under the couch, only to find nothing. I slowly stood up from the couch, walked to the enclosed front porch that borders the living room, peeked around the corner, but again, saw nothing more. This little creature went as quickly and as suddenly as it came.

One can try to convince oneself, and others can try to convince you, that perhaps what you've seen was just your imagination, and possibly just a dream. This was no dream. I know what I saw was real because there have been too many other unexplained paranormal activities in this house and in other homes and elsewhere in my lifetime that I, as well as others, have experienced. (I may just write my own book one of these days!)

The Ghost Cat of King John's Hunting Lodge

by Gerina Dunwich

K ing John's Hunting Lodge in the small English village of Axbridge is a timber-framed Tudor building that dates back to the sixteenth century. It is currently owned by the National Trust and used as a museum of local history and archaeology. A paneled room located on the first floor of this medieval building is reputed to be haunted by the mysterious ghosts of a tabby cat and an Elizabethan woman, who has come to be known as the White Lady.

On August 22, 1978, two people claimed to have seen the White Lady sitting in a chair in the paneled room. Their report was recorded in the museum's diary. No sightings of the White Lady have since been reported.

The cat apparition, on the other hand, continues to make appearances from time to time and is usually seen after dark and at the top of the stairs. A number of individuals have also sighted it entering the paneled room through a closed door. On one occasion, the feline stirred up quite a commotion when it entered the room while a lecture was in progress. Witnesses reported seeing it sit down and curl its tail around its paw before vanishing into thin air.

A spiritualist medium that visited the museum verified the hauntings and claimed the room where the sightings of the White Lady and the cat took place possessed a violent past.

The Haunted Cottage

by Eileen Smith

I rented an old cottage on an inlet in Point Pleasant, New Jersey. At night I always sat in this one chair to read or watch TV. At the same time each night, around 9 or 10, I had this incredible strong feeling that something had walked up behind my chair and was standing very close behind my left shoulder. So strong was this feeling that if I turned around I thought for sure I would see someone there.

My cat Amber, who has since passed on, was at the time plump and a little on the lazy side, very loving but not particularly playful. I noticed her sudden interest in the upstairs attic, which looked as if it at some time had served as a loft or bedroom. She also began to play for hours and hours with what I could only describe as a "playmate." She would run after it, and then act like she was being playfully chased. She would do this all night long, especially on the stairs to the walk-up attic.

I then began to experience the sounds of a cat's meow, which was very faint. I also saw what appeared to be a black-and-white cat in the corner of my eye. I discussed this with my husband at the time (we have since parted) and he told me he saw this cat, too!

My husband worked very late at night, and one time at 3 a.m. he needed to get a tool from the attic. He told me the next morning that he'd seen the reflecting eyes of a cat shining back at him while he was up there.

One night I awoke to see the figure of a woman in a dress (circa 1919) standing at the foot of the bed. This sounds rather fantastic, but it was just the body in the dress; I did not see the head. This did not frighten me for some reason. I really think these two ghosts rather liked us being there.

I became extremely creative and content in that house. Its energy was such that I wrote a children's book and began to paint for the first time (I now am an active artist) and painted what I feel is probably one of my best works to date.

On the day my husband and I moved out, as it was just a winter rental, the ghost cat was seen constantly by both of us, just sitting in the middle of the room, or on the windowsills, watching, as if to say it knew we were moving and was sad to see us leave. I only wish we could have taken it with us.

Yellow Kitty

by Tonya Brooks

I have always been close to animals and feel I have a special way of communicating with them. I have also experienced my "babies" coming back after death to let me know they are all right.

Nine years ago my boyfriend Paul and I started rescuing animals. Our first rescue was a big yellow tomcat that we named Yellow Kitty. It took us five months to build a bond with him because he was hurt. I suspected his injuries were inflicted by humans, but I did not know for sure.

We captured him one day to get him to the vet because the wounds were becoming infected. We found out that he had feline immunodeficiency virus (FIV), but we didn't give up on him. We took him back to our house and he became such a loving cat. You could hear him purr from across the room.

He became very ill one night and we rushed him to the vet, but there was nothing that could be done for him. He was too dehydrated and in pain, so we had to have him put to sleep. He died in my arms, looking into my eyes as I told him that I loved him. We then took him home and buried him.

Within a couple of days I had my first encounter with his spirit, and so did Paul. I was sleeping on the couch and awoke to the feeling of a cat kneading my stomach. There was no cat there, at least not physically. I started to tell Paul about it the next day but he beat me to it and told me he had the same experience.

I believe Yellow Kitty was letting us know that he was all right and still with us, that he loved us and was grateful for the love that we had given to him.

Unfortunately, through the years many of the animals that we rescued died, but the experiences live on. My angels (as I call them) have touched my heart and my spirit. I still feel their presence with me; they like to jump into bed with me every now and then. Tipper, my cat, sleeps with me every night and gets upset when they decide to visit.

Callie

by C. A. Banks

Callie came into our lives the Christmas season of 1984. A neighbor gave her to my then three-year-old daughter for a present. Callie was only a kitten, but there was a sweet, matronly aspect to her even then. If she had been a person, I would have pictured her to be a slightly plump brunette woman, who loved to feed and nurture those who were close to her.

Callie quickly learned to love the outdoors. We lived on the outskirts of town, and there were plenty of fields and wooded areas for her to explore. She frequently gifted me with dead mice, gophers, and once, unfortunately, a baby bunny.

The most outstanding thing about Callie was her amazing spiritual and magickal ability. I often found her meditating, facing east. She often appeared in my dreams when they became frightening. She was always close by when I prayed or when I performed a healing ritual for a friend.

She divided her nights between my daughter's bedroom and mine. At some point in the night, Callie would gracefully leap up onto the bed, landing on my shoulder and walking down the length of my body. I drowsily scolded her for waking me, but I loved when she lay against my legs and purred. It was as if she were watching over us. She was fiercely loyal and protective of my daughter and me.

Once, when Callie was out, a bat got in the house, badly frightening us. A neighbor came and took the bat away, but the next morning the bat was found dead on the front porch. Its ears were chewed off.

The most significant event in our eleven years with Callie was the time I saw an apparition in my bedroom. I had awoken to go to the bathroom. I was returning to my bedroom, foggy with sleep, when I noticed that Callie was crouched in the doorway, ears flattened, staring intently into the room. This was so unlike her that I was disturbed. I entered the room cautiously and looked around, suspecting some form of wildlife. Seeing nothing, I climbed back into bed. That was when I noticed a young man kneeling next to my exercise bike. He looked as if he were lit from within. I could see through him to the wall behind him. He wore a white shirt, dark slacks, and a sort of windbreaker jacket. He was smiling.

I screamed and ran into my daughter's room. Callie remained crouching in the doorway, staring. (Any suspicion that I might be imagining the whole thing was dispelled by the cat's obvious perception of the same thing I was seeing.) My daughter awoke and I held her, shaking uncontrollably.

Finally, I called an acquaintance who happened to be a professional psychic, and she told me that this person meant no harm but had come to warn me about something. Later, my daughter's bike was stolen. I guess the ghost was trying to warn us about that.

We moved away, shortly after that, back into the city. Callie didn't adjust very well to the move. At night, I heard her meowing mournfully. She still shared her nights equally between my daughter and I.

One day, I found a lump on her abdomen. I took her to the vet and learned that Callie had cancer. Although we had the tumor removed, she soon developed three more. As she grew weaker, I knew we had to let Callie go. I had a long talk with my daughter, and then we explained our decision to Callie. I knew that she understood. The next day I drove her to the Humane Society to be euthanized. As they carried her pet carrier away, she winked at me.

We moved out of state after that.

One night, about two years later, I was grieving for Callie. I wept a little and then fell asleep. At one point during the night I awoke. My eyes were closed but I could see the wall behind the bed begin to glow with a bright light. It seemed to dissolve into a mist and then Callie gracefully jumped through it. She landed on my shoulder and walked across my stomach exactly the way she had every single night in her life. I drowsily started to scold her, just the way

I had countless times before. Then a feeling of such overwhelming grief and love overcame me that my eyes filled with tears again.

I opened my eyes. I couldn't see her, but I could feel her little paws as she began walking along my body toward the foot of the bed as she always did in the past. She plopped down and began to purr. I lay very still, scarcely breathing. I could feel the purrs vibrating along my leg, just as always!

That loving visit healed me of my grief. It was proof to me that my Callie still lived on, just on another plane of existence. By the end of that year, our next cat came into our lives.

In Dreams Comes the Cat

by Selma Sanchez

Gigi and I were the best of friends. I adopted her from the local animal shelter when she was just a kitten. With orange and brown stripes that made her resemble a little tiger and the most adorable green eyes I'd ever seen on a cat, it was a classic case of love at first sight!

Gigi was a sweetheart. She was a gentle and loving cat with the best of manners. But she also had a lot of energy and loved to play. The first toy I bought her was a little catnip-filled mouse on a string. I would make the mouse move by pulling on the string and she would wildly chase after it, catch it, and wrestle around with it. It was her favorite toy to play with, but one day it just disappeared. I didn't know if Gigi hid it, or if it had gotten caught under a piece of furniture. I searched high and low but was never able to find it. Its disappearance was a mystery.

Gigi and I shared seven wonderful years together until one fateful day when a liver tumor took her from me. The vet had done all that he could to help my little tiger, but it was to no avail.

For weeks after Gigi's death I thought about her and missed her so much I broke down and cried. During this time of grieving I also made the saddening discovery that people who never had an emotional bond with a pet were incapable of understanding the deep sadness and feeling of loss that a person experiences after losing a pet that was dear to them. In many ways it's comparable to losing a close friend or even one of your children.

At the factory where I work, a coworker who noticed that I seemed a bit down asked me what was wrong. When I told her that my cat had recently passed away, she acted kind of annoyed and coldly told me to "just get over it and buy yourself another cat." One friend told me she couldn't understand my sorrow because, after all, it "wasn't like a person had died." Remarks such as these only added anger to my grief, and gave me a sense of isolation. Perhaps I did grieve for Gigi a little longer than the socially accepted time period allows for grieving the death of a pet. But she was a very special part of my life, and I took her death quite hard.

After my emotional healing process began and I could get through the day without tears, Gigi began coming to me in my dreams. She appeared as she looked when she first came into my life—a young and healthy kitten, loving and playful. At first I thought the dreams were just my mind's way of keeping Gigi's memory alive. But then something peculiar happened.

One night I dreamed that Gigi, again as a kitten, was playing with me on my bed. I was making scratching sounds with my fingertips under the blanket and she was pouncing on it, just as she had done so many times when she was alive. I then took her in my arms and cuddled and kissed her. I told her I loved her and that she was my little tiger. The dream was vivid and seemed so real that when I awoke, I felt for a few moments that Gigi was still alive. But as soon as I remembered she had died, I felt the tears well up in my eyes. I got up and went into the bathroom to wash my face and brush my teeth, and when I looked in the mirror, that's when I noticed there was a bit of cat hair stuck to my flannel nightgown. It was Gigi's hair. In an effort to be as rational as possible, I tried to convince myself that this was just a highly unusual coincidence. But then another dream convinced me otherwise.

One Sunday afternoon I was watching television in my living room and started to feel drowsy. I drifted off to sleep on the sofa and dreamed that Gigi was running around the room playing with her favorite catnip mouse. She was having fun with the toy and I was enjoying watching her play. When I woke up, I noticed something across the room on the floor. I got up and went over for a closer look and it was Gigi's catnip mouse—the one that had been missing for years!

I instantly took this as a sign that her spirit had, in some unexplained way, been paying visits to me while I was in the dream state. I felt no fear that she had returned from the dead. In fact, I took great comfort in knowing that she isn't really gone; she lives on in the spirit world.

I've told this story to my family and some of my friends and most think I'm either making it up, imagining it, or just plain *loco*. I know what I experienced, and it doesn't really matter to me if they believe it or not.

Gigi and I were the best of friends. And we still are.

A Ghostly Encounter with Tiger

by Robin Johnsen-Malone

About a year ago my husband, Dave, and I were due to go to England for a much needed trip. My husband, who was born in the U.K., was looking forward to visiting his parents and other family members.

We were informed that his childhood cat, Tiger, was quite ill. He was an old cat, quite friendly except when the children were around; then he would leg it (a British expression meaning "run away").

It used to be quite amusing when we visited because on the first day of our arrival Tiger would come to greet us, but after that we would rarely see him. Every now and again he jumped up on your lap when he felt that the coast was clear. When we received the call that he was put to sleep we weren't surprised. My husband was quite sad because he grew up with this kitty and loved him deeply.

Not long after, we boarded the plane for England and arrived early in the morning. As usual we were quite tired. My husband's parents picked us up and whisked us off to their beautiful home in the north of England situated in an area called the Wirral.

The house they live in is very old. In fact, it was a manor house back in the day and the land was subsequently built on to provide housing for families. Needless to say the house is quite old and at night especially you can hear a lot of creaking and groaning.

A few days later I was sipping my morning coffee with Dave's mother. After reminiscing about our numerous trips here and there, I excused myself to check my e-mail. The computer was housed in the guest area of the house, which is attached but very separate from the main house. I headed toward the room feeling the damp cold air chill me to the bone. I hugged myself extra tight because living in a warm climate can make you more prone to getting cold.

I pulled the chair out from the desk where the computer was sitting and started checking mail from my friends. The door was right next to where I was sitting. In fact, I could reach out my arm and touch it, so it didn't surprise me at all when the door started to open a bit. I figured there was a draft somewhere and didn't think anything of it.

All of a sudden, out of the corner of my eye I saw a cat brush up against the side of the doorjamb and glide into the room. And as quickly as it came in, it vanished. I sat up quickly and rubbed my eyes a few times and then I whispered, "Tiger is that you?" but he never reappeared.

But I know what I saw and I quickly reported it to my in-laws who didn't seem too surprised. They sometimes felt his presence but had not seen him. They said that they were delighted to know that I had seen him and from then on we would reminisce about good old Tiger who would run hiding at the first sign of small feet pattering on the floor.

Good old Tiger. He's still alive and kicking.

The Conjured Cat

by Lisa Abney

One night my husband and I performed a ritual in our back-yard. While raising our energy and casting our circle, I asked him if he had felt anything looking in on our circle. He said he could, and we both figured, well that's what we wanted, right? Well, in the middle of our ritual, he looked down and saw a cat rubbing up against his legs. Mind you, this was definitely *not* one of our cats. After a little time went by, the cat started rubbing against my legs and feet. Not bothered by our visitor, we continued to finish our ritual.

Afterward, we went into the house to have cakes and ale (which, in all honesty, were Oreos and sparkling apple cider). As we stood there talking, we both noticed that our circle guest was in the house. The same lanky black cat that had joined us in our circle bolted through our kitchen and into the dining room. So, naturally, we went to look for it.

We both looked under and around our dining room table, but we saw nothing. So we continued looking all around the house—the bedrooms, closets, living room, laundry room, and back to the kitchen. We both eventually met up in the bathroom. I asked my husband if he had seen the cat and he said no. So, after checking the bathtub, I closed the bathroom door to check the closet, which is in the same corner as the door.

As I stood there making sure I wasn't about to lock some poor cat into my tiny linen closet, out of the corner of my eye I saw the bathroom door crack open. The black cat coolly walked into the room and came right over to me. Again it started rubbing up against me, letting me know it was friendly.

I called my husband into the room. He came in and pushed the door open the rest of the way. We both stood there greeting this mysterious animal and trying to actually pet it when it suddenly darted out of the room. As my husband and I followed the cat, we saw it round the corner for the kitchen. We both came around the corner to find the kitchen empty, so I stood there in the doorway to make sure the cat didn't get past while my husband searched the kitchen. Needless to say, we found nothing, not even a cracked door or open window to the outside. Our friendly little visitor had vanished.

Nevertheless, every time my husband and I perform a ritual in our circle, we can feel the presence of this animal. Whether it is a guardian, a totem, or a spirit, it was one of the most magickal experiences of my life.

Frolic

by Tara Fischbach

In my home in Federal Way, Washington, we always had cats. We loved them so much that when my dad found abandoned kittens in a parking lot the whole family gladly spent the time to bottle-feed and raise them.

Over the years we owned a lot of different kitties because, unfortunately, we lived with a busy street on one side of our house, woods on the other, and woods across the street, which all made for a bad combination concerning curious cats. My dad, however, had a cat that was smart and tuff, Pig Pen (she got this name because the first day we had her she racked up the garage and got filthy). She was just a little too "friendly" with the tomcats in our neighborhood and was always pregnant.

One summer Pig Pen had a fairly large litter, eight kittens. I went out to the garage, her favorite nesting place, and brought her fresh food and water every day. I also checked on the kittens to make sure they were doing all right as well.

The first day I went out I heard a kitten's faint "meow" away from the litter, but couldn't find it. A little over a week passed by and one day when I checked on Pig Pen I definitely heard a kitten on the other side of the garage. I searched all through a bunch of stored boxes and found him. He was much smaller than all the other kittens, had bugs crawling on him, and was very weak. I rushed into the house, cleaned him up, and checked him over. I could tell he was very malnourished because his gums were white. I showed my dad and cried, asking if we could get him some kitten formula so I could take care of him. My dad, of course, said yes.

I raised that kitten on my own; he was all mine. I immediately had a special bond with him and kept him with me all the time. He slept in my bedroom in his own little basket, went with me when I went to my friends' homes, and was like a baby to me. When he began walking he had a funny little hop to him. To me he seemed to frolic around, so that is what I named him, Frolic.

I soon learned the reason he was abandoned; he seemed to be mentally retarded. With so many kittens to feed, Pig Pen must have taken the "defective" one and disposed of it. Frolic would fall off of ledges, walk into walls, and literally trip over his own feet. I desperately tried to keep him inside but being a male cat, that was impossible.

Frolic came up missing for a few days and I found him in the woods by our house. I could see a car had hit him; his tail was limp and he could barely move. I nursed him back to health and again a car hit him. He survived the second one but you know what they say: "Third time's a charm."

I came home one night with a new collar for Frolic and my dad looked sad when I showed the collar to him. I had had Frolic for three years, raised him myself, nursed him back to health twice, and loved him more than anything, so my dad knew the sensitivity of the news he was about to tell me. He sat me down and said he found Frolic dead by the road when he got home from work and buried him. I cried so much it was like having my heart ripped out.

That night I went to bed and dreamed that Frolic came up from the grave to see me. The next night I had the same dream. On the third night I was settling in and felt something jump on the bed and settle in just like Frolic would do. I moved my feet around thinking it was my imagination, settled in again, and felt the same movement at my feet. I jumped up and turned on the light, but nothing was there. I got back into bed and again felt him jump up on the bed and lay down at my feet where he always did. I just let it go and went to sleep.

I told my mom about it the next day and she said he probably came in like he always did. I thought it was kind of strange that there could be a ghost cat. I thought only people became ghosts, but my mom explained that he was my baby and probably wasn't ready to go.

One night I had a bad dream and awoke startled. It felt like I kicked something and heard his telltale "meow." Every night for months I felt him snuggle up to my feet. It was nice to have him around a little longer and it made his passing a little easier to bear.

I think maybe he somehow knew how much I loved him and wanted to stick around just a little while longer.

My Ethereal Feline Encounter

(anonymous)

My family had a cat named Tuffy from March 24, 1978, to March 28, 2000. Tuffy was a ginger tabby with looks similar to Morris the 9 Lives cat, but with less white. He came into the family from a coworker at the oil company where my dad worked. On our own, we had been unable to find another ginger tabby to replace an older cat that had to be put to sleep. This coworker mentioned he had a tabby kitten in his cat's litter. We met Tuffy and he went home with us.

Tuffy and I grew up together. After the Yorkshire terrier came into the family, Tuffy used my room as a refuge from the terror (err . . . terrier). Tuffy was always protective of me to the point where he once ran off a high school boyfriend of mine. After I moved away, Tuffy and I spent plenty of quality time together when I came home to visit. On the morning of March 28, 2000, the same day a tornado struck downtown Fort Worth, Tuffy died.

Flash-forward to Friday, March 18, 2004, at my apartment in southern New Mexico. . . . I usually speak to my parents on Fridays in the late afternoon and was expecting their call. Around five o'clock, I turned around and saw a ghostly image of Tuffy in the blue butterfly chair in my living room. I tried to reach out and touch him and he made a hissing reaction, but with no sound. Then he was gone. Two hours later, I looked over at the chair and he was there again with a scared expression. He vanished within a second or two of me seeing him. I tried calling home but got no answer.

Around ten o'clock that night, my mother called to let me know that my father had been hospitalized following an accident. I told her that I knew something had happened when Tuffy appeared. She wasn't surprised since things like this are known to happen on her side of the family.

The Haunted Hospital

by Gerina Dunwich

Ghost sightings at hospitals and other medical facilities are not unusual occurrences because these are places where many people have suffered in pain and have met with death. However, the sightings of ghostly animals at such places (other than veterinary hospitals) are not all that common.

At the Tucson Medical Center in Arizona, some folks have seen a ghostly black cat roaming the halls at various hours of the day and night. When attempts are made to corner and catch it, the phantom feline does a vanishing act by running through walls.

Some staff members and patients alike have also reported seeing the apparitions of a woman in black and a child who disappears through walls and closed doors. Many believe that these are the ghosts of former patients who died there.

It is not known whether there exists any connection between the black cat and the child and the woman in black. And to this day it remains a mystery why the animal haunts the hospital. Perhaps it was once the loving pet of a now-deceased patient or staff member and, having passed on itself, is simply searching for its long lost human companion to reunite with.

Tortured Souls

by Mary Beth Reisner

In September of 1988 my husband and I, along with our six-year-old daughter, Stacey, moved into a rented three-bedroom Cape Cod–style house in a quiet residential neighborhood outside of Milwaukee.

The first night we spent in the house we were awakened around 1 a.m. by the sound of our little girl sobbing loudly. I got out of bed and went to Stacey's room to see why she was crying. I found her sitting up in her bed, clutching one of her stuffed animals, and looking terrified. She told me she had been frightened by the sight of a strange animal moving around in her room. She thought it was a large white cat with yellow glowing eyes, but she wasn't sure because it didn't have a tail. I reassured her that it was just a bad dream, then sat with her until she went back to sleep.

A few days later my husband had a strange experience while working downstairs in the basement. Something caught his eye and he looked up to see a large white cat with blood trickling from its nostrils peering in at him from the basement window. In a matter of seconds the cat's image faded away before his eyes. He felt sure he had just imagined it and thought our daughter's earlier "bad dream" about a white cat was purely coincidental.

Several weeks passed without anything out of the ordinary

happening in the house. Halloween arrived and my husband and I took Stacey trick-or-treating around the neighborhood. As we returned home we all spotted what appeared to be a white cat sitting in the upstairs window of Stacey's bedroom. My daughter immediately became terrified and said she didn't want to sleep in that room anymore because she was afraid the "spooky cat" would get her. We checked Stacey's room for the cat but found nothing. My husband then searched the entire house from top to bottom. No cat.

We invited relatives over for Thanksgiving dinner, and I nearly choked on my food when one of my husband's elderly aunts asked him what our cat's name was! He told her we didn't own a cat, and she replied that that was odd because she was sure she had seen a cat in the hallway earlier when she went to freshen up in the bathroom. I asked her if the cat she saw happened to be a big white one with a missing tail, and she gave me a bewildered look and laughed. The cat she had seen was a little striped tabby. She added that it was a "shy puss" because it took off running as soon as it saw her. We all laughed and joked about the mystery cat, but somehow I couldn't help feel in my heart that there was something disturbing about these strange cat sightings.

One day I was outside chatting with our next-door neighbor, Connie. She was filling me in on all the neighborhood gossip, so I asked her what the previous tenants who occupied our house were like. She replied that the Housers were a nice older couple who were quiet and mostly kept to themselves. I then asked Connie if they had any cats, and she shook her head no. She said they had a couple of pet birds, parakeets or canaries; she wasn't sure which.

She then said, "It's a funny thing that you mentioned cats because the family that lived there before the Housers had a teenage son who was nothing but a little monster. He got his kicks from torturing stray cats."

I felt nauseous as she told me a story about how her husband once caught this obviously disturbed young man trying to hang a kitten by its neck from the clothesline in the backyard.

That night I lit a candle and said a special prayer for all the cats and kittens that had been tortured and killed at the hands of the cruel boy who once lived in the house that my family now called home. It must have done some good, because we continued to live in the house for another year and a half without experiencing any further incidents of feline hauntings; I'm now convinced that's what they were.

The Legend of the Cat Lady

by Maureen Gabrinetti

A strange story about a cat lady was told to me when I was a young girl growing up in an Irish immigrant neighborhood in south Boston. I don't know how much of it is fact and how much is urban legend, but the person who told it to me swore on a Holy Bible that it was the God's honest truth.

The story goes that there was this elderly woman in the neighborhood who lived by herself in an old shabby house. She was a recluse and seldom ventured out of her home. Some say it was because she didn't like or trust other people. She did, however, have quite a fondness for cats and took in every stray cat and kitten that wandered into her backyard until her house was overrun with felines.

Many of the neighborhood children were afraid of the cat lady and some believed she was a witch. All sorts of weird rumors were spread about her, even among some of the adults, and on every Halloween the nasty little trick-or-treaters would bombard this woman's house with stones and apples and then run off into the shadows of the night as fast as they could.

When the cat lady died, her body wasn't discovered until about a week later. By that time, the horde of hungry cats that were trapped inside the house without any food had devoured much of the old woman's flesh. She was so badly eaten that the authorities had to use dental records to properly identify her.

Animal control officers rounded up all of the cats. Some of them had diseases and infections from being in catfights, and some were downright vicious. All of them were destroyed. Afterward, the house was cleaned out and put up for sale by a relative.

It was about two years later when the house, which was still vacant, mysteriously burned to the ground. Although no one was ever charged with arson, it was rumored that some of the neighbors banded together and torched the house because they believed it was haunted by the ghosts of the old lady and her cats and was bringing bad luck to the families in the neighborhood.

A few years after this story was told to me, I heard a slightly different version from someone else. They claimed the reason the old lady's house had been set ablaze was because some of the more superstitious people in the neighborhood believed that because the cats had eaten part of the woman's body, their ghosts returned as demons every Samhain eve (October 31) to feed upon more human flesh.

JoJo, Uncle Willard, and Me

by Lee Prosser

One of my most unusual ghostly encounters involved a petite black cat with green eyes. Her name was JoJo, and she belonged to Willard David Firestone, an uncle of mine who lived with me in Missouri until his death from cancer in 1979.

Uncle Willard was a composer and pianist and played one of the best forms of stride piano around. He was also an adept of many occult systems of magick and taught them to me. There was an incredible, enduring bond between JoJo and Uncle Willard, and the cat oftentimes accompanied him on walks. She was also the guard cat of the house, so to speak.

By the spring of 1989, JoJo had developed a form of eye cancer, which spread rapidly. She had the charming habit of coming up on the edge of my bed and purring loudly as she watched me awake. JoJo's one good eye was always full of mischief and humor, as if to say, the cancer got the other one and turned it cloudy but this one still has blue skies for seeing!

Late one night I thought I heard JoJo cry, but when I turned on the light there was no sign of her. In the morning I awoke to find her lifeless body hanging on the edge of the bed. Dying, she had made it to the right corner of the bed and sunk her claws into the bedding. Her head was on the mattress, both eyes staring toward me. That big blind eye seemed larger than usual. I took her from the bed, said a special prayer for her, and buried her quietly within the hour.

Four days later JoJo came back to visit me. I had been listening to classical music by Antonio Vivaldi, an Italian composer. It was nearing midnight and I went to bed. I recall sensing a presence close to me, and it woke me. I turned on the nightstand light and got out of bed. The room seemed abnormally quiet, as if within a deep peaceful slumber. I went into the kitchen, got a small glass of cool water, drank it, and went back to my bedroom. On the right corner of the bed sat the spirits of my Uncle Willard and his cat JoJo. The cat now had two good eyes and seemed delighted to see me. Uncle Willard was as I recalled him: white-haired and muscular, a wiry man with a lot of magick inside him.

The image of these two ghosts before me was clear and lasted a full moment. It was a beautiful moment for me. Uncle Willard and JoJo, united again in a world without pain and in a world without sorrow. I honored their presence with a deeply thought wave of love, sweeping out from me to them, and I felt that love return with equal kindness and joy. Then as if to signal good-bye, JoJo flicked her tail and Uncle Willard smiled. They vanished.

To this day, I cherish the memory of both, and it was a wonderful way of sharing with me the truth that death is only another beginning to a new journey in the afterlife. The memory of this ghostly encounter is as vivid today as it was when it happened.

Roz and Wiz

by Lee Prosser

In the year 2004, I lost two of my beloved cats, Roz and Wiz. They were a true cat couple, and they were always together. Roz was a large mixture of Burmese and Abyssinian, and she loved to play. Wiz was a shy male, large, a mixture of Siamese and

Abyssinian. They came out of the same household from different litters. They were both born at Roswell, New Mexico. Roz and Wiz were not old when they died months apart. They both died of pancreatic cancer.

Through 2005 they would return to play on the edge of the bed, or brush by my face. They were always loving, remembering my love for them and sharing their love for me. Now they are playing in the afterlife, somewhere in time, enjoying the fine art of being a cat in each one's own personal way.

At times, I can sense their presence from a far distance, and I smile and remember their love and the joyful playfulness they brought into my life. When I think of the state of New Mexico and its land of enchantment, I will always recall Roz and Wiz and be thankful they were part of my life.

The Coming

by Lee Prosser

It was January 19, 2005, and I was sitting on the couch at my home in Oklahoma reading a John Steinbeck novel, *To a God Unknown*. My two Siamese cats, Frank and Barry, were curled up asleep in my lap.

It seemed that time slowed and there was a strange, unusual quietness in the living room. The cats awoke and got off of my lap. They went to the hallway, sat on the carpet, and stared at something. I got up, but I did not see anything unusual. As I started back to the couch, I paused and sensed the coming of something.

Something was coming.

I turned around and saw the ghost of Roz, my departed cat. She was just sitting there, and she appeared to be communicating with Frank and Barry. I called her name, and she heard me. Roz did a little dance, turned, and vanished. The Siamese cats looked at me and returned to the couch. I joined them.

Roz had dropped by to say hello, and it was a welcome visit. Cats have souls and a sense of remembrance, and they never forget those they love and who love them.

The Ghosts of the Snuggly Kitties

by Melissa Morris

This is a story of what turned out to be a great comfort to my sister. She and I have always believed that those who have passed before us, human and animal, may have occasion to visit from time to time.

She and her husband had just bought their first house together. Her husband worked third shift, which left her to spend many nights alone. She was a little concerned because before she and her husband were married, she had suffered a late-night break-in at her previous place of residence. Needless to say, spending nights alone was not her cup of tea.

During her first week at the new house, she decided she would work on her skills of controlling her fears through mind power. She would simply convince herself that she was safe and there was nothing to be afraid of. But, to her dismay, she had a terrible time going to sleep and often would get up and go into the living room, turn on the TV, and fall asleep on the couch.

Finally, after a few weeks of backaches and stiff joints, she decided to tackle the bed again. She decided that no matter what, she was going to get in that bed and sleep in it all night. With this new-found sense of courage and determination, she shut out the light, crawled in the bed, and (against every fiber of her being) turned off the comforting night-light.

Within minutes, she was startled by the sensation of something small jumping on the bed and walking up toward her head. Moving at the speed of sound, she jumped up, flipped on the light, and picked up her hairbrush, ready to take out the intruder trying to be her bedfellow. But, nothing was there. Nothing! Quite disturbed at this point, more at herself than anything, she turned off the light and got back in bed. Again, thump, and then pitter-patter up the side of the bed. And, once again, she was up out of the bed, lights blazing, eyes wide, sweat beading, and hands shaking. *Sure it's possible to imagine something once, but twice?* Thoroughly shaken now, she grabbed her pillow and blanket and retreated to the couch.

The next day, she decided to contact the seller of the house to inquire of his knowledge of these occurrences. To her surprise, he actually found the incident quite humorous. She, however, had not yet seen the hilarity of the situation. The gentleman went on to explain that the house had actually belonged to his mother and that she had lived there for the better part of fifty years. She also had a great love of cats! Many a kitty had lived long happy lives in that house and had succumbed to old age snuggled up beside their beloved caretaker. She had, in fact, mentioned to her son that she felt her feline friends would still pay visits to her, looking for her comfort and kindness. She always invited them up on the bed. After all, that's where they loved to be anyway.

Armed with this new piece of knowledge, my sister decided that her visitors were indeed friends—not enemies. That night, she crawled in bed again—still a little apprehensive. And yet again, she felt the now familiar thump and then little feet walking up the bed. This time, she didn't panic. She just remained still, speaking softly to her little friend. A few minutes later, she felt another thump and more feet. She said that she felt there were probably four or five little visitors that night. They simply found a place to nest, and then were still.

They came back the next night, and the night after. Pretty soon, my sister began to look forward to their company. They provided a great comfort to her while her husband was at work. In fact, the little guys lulled her to sleep with their little kitty snuggles.

The Cat in the Dumbwaiter

by Andi Jennifer Sowers

In an old apartment building, once a classy hotel in downtown Miami, I made my home on the ninth floor with my boyfriend. With one bedroom, a small galley-size kitchen, and two windows facing the harbor, our lives were compacted into a tiny area. Over several decades, many people have shared this room, their memories and lives stained into the walls around me. I pondered if this place was a hotbed for spirits, paranormal energy, or ghostly sightings. Curiously, there would only be a pleasant silence and a peaceful setting to call home. Until one day, a faint cry was heard from the wall of my bedroom.

During the sweltering heat of a hot summer day, I was thankful that I had the day off from work. Since I had an obsession with saving money, going out into town for some south Florida fun was out of the question. So, I decided to finish reading my favorite novel, *Haunted,* by Tamara Thorne. As I lay comfortably in my bed with satin sheets and a fan silently blowing, a small slightly muted sound emanated from my bedroom wall. I paused a moment, looking above the pages of my paperback, observing the usual scenery of my cluttered space. Must have been something on the street far below, I thought, and returned to my book.

"Mew."

My wall spoke more clearly, causing me to cautiously look up a second time. Butterflies rose in my stomach as I recognized the sound. *Is there a cat behind the wall?* My neighbors had moved out two months ago. They had never mentioned having pets. I crept up to the wall slowly, not knowing what to expect. My horror novel must have added some anxiety to the situation.

"Mew."

I paused, not moving a muscle. Okay, I thought, maybe there is a cat stuck in the empty apartment next door. I threw on some decent clothes and headed downstairs to the office. Luckily one of my friends was manning the desk. I told him about the situation, and he accompanied me back up to the ninth floor to investigate the mysterious cat crying for help.

The apartment next door was what I expected, empty and damp from the midsummer weather. But to my surprise, no cat was found. My friend thought I heard it from the street below. I didn't feel like arguing, especially over a cat that wasn't around. So, I nodded in agreement. Before our departure from the vacant apartment, I noticed a crease in the shared wall. It was badly cracked and sunken in. Not saying anything about it to my friend, I returned to my room.

I immediately went to the mysterious mewing wall and studied the structure of it. I noticed a crease running vertically from the ceiling to the floor, much like the other side, only not as many signs of damage. I knelt down to study the bottom half of the floorboard, when I noticed a small hole. Ignoring all the advice of every horror novel ever written, I tugged on the small board. It loosened! I quickly grabbed a screwdriver to help pry the old board and with a little strength, I pulled it completely up. Anxiously, I grabbed my flashlight and peered into the darkness. Looking straight down, I saw another floorboard one foot down. I assumed that it was a support for the flooring I normally walked on. I then shined my flashlight diagonally expecting to find the wall continuing down, but to my surprise, it was an open space that extended outward. This wall was concealing what appeared to be a small shaft of some sort. I barely contained my excitement and retrieved a mirror from my bathroom. Again, ignoring the laws of every blood-curdling horror novel, I stuck the mirror inside the dark space aiming my flashlight to enhance the reflection. It indeed was a shaft no wider than a couple of feet. *Wow, it must be an old dumbwaiter from back in the days when this building was a hotel,* I thought. I angled the mirror downward to see how long it was. It didn't go down very far, and to my shock, there was something at the bottom.

My hand began to shake as I tried to change the angle of light in order to get a full picture of my discovery. A small incomplete skeleton was lying at the bottom of the shaft. Despite my lack of lighting, I could make out a few small clumps of matted fur around dry bones and the top of a tiny skull. My anxiety transformed into fascination of what was entombed beneath my small apartment I called home. I wished I could see the front of the tiny head to help in my speculation as to whether it was indeed a cat.

I'm a natural skeptic. I never knew if the poor animal was actually a cat, nor if the sound of the mewing actually came from the spirit of this skeleton, but I felt that this little creature in its final resting place deserved some words of peace. Though I lacked any experience with the other side, I decided to grab some rose petals from my bouquet next to the window, gently dropping them into the tomb while whispering words of comfort. I replaced the top floorboard, never to open it again.

Up until I moved away to a new house, I always kept listening, wondering if I would ever hear the faint cry of a cat again. I heard only silence.

Saboochi's Return

(anonymous)

Each evening my daughter's beloved cat (whom she named Saboochi) followed her into her bedroom and began the night by sleeping with her. But at some point in the middle of the night Saboochi always transferred herself to our room for the reminder of her sleep.

In our bedroom we have a very large set of clothing drawers that are built into the wall and roll out via wheels in a track. For years Saboochi had mastered the art of jumping up, catching her claws on the lip of the highest drawer, hanging there, and, in so doing, having the weight of her body enable the drawer to roll out away from the wall. She would then hoist herself up and over and into the drawer where she would settle in to sleep for the rest of the night. In the morning we would awake, lift her out, and close the drawer. It was a well-established routine.

About seven years ago, Saboochi was hit by a car and killed in front of our home. A couple of nights after she died, I was awakened in the night by the sound of the drawer rolling out. But I was so sleepy it was not enough to make me sit up and take notice . . . after all, it was a part of the sounds in our house for so long. The next morning, I found the drawer open when I got up and asked my husband if he had heard what I heard. He had, and neither one of us blinked an eye at the drawer being open, preferring to think that our kitty was simply letting us know that she was still around. It happened on another night that week, too, and then no more.

It gave great comfort to our daughter, who was about eleven at the time, to know that Saboochi was still in our house. She experienced a feeling of pressure on her body and the bed covers like her kitty was curling up to sleep with her.

I've also had the experience of hearing my dog, Aja, walking across the tile floor, her nails clicking on the surface as she went, long after her death. I've also heard the jingle bell attached to her collar.

More than one psychic has told me that they have received information from the other side that we are reunited with our pets when we cross over. I'd like to believe that's true.

Tigger

by Laura Maxwell

Our cat, Tigger, disappeared sometime ago. My husband and I thought nothing of it until after a couple of days because he was an outside cat. We went out looking for him and he would not come to my call or anything, which was not like him.

It wasn't until later when I went out looking for him again that I found him. I called to him and went to pick him up, but he disappeared. That's when I knew he was dead.

Every now and then when I'm looking for something I still hear him meow like he's trying to get my attention. I even feel him now and then rub himself against my leg when my mind is wandering. At night I often feel a cat sleeping on me or at my feet. Or I hear purring. I get up and look because we don't allow cats in our room because of our new baby. And there is nothing there.

Also, in the morning my husband will go to the car and see cat paw prints. We know they're Tigger's because he had a very distinct paw pattern and a cut on his back leg paw, and we saw this in one of the paw prints.

Now and then we see my cat Athena playing with something that's not there. We believe it's Tigger because he was the only cat she would play with. And sometimes we see cat eyes staring at us at night outside and when we go to see what it is, there's nothing there.

Whenever we see something like a cat or hear a cat we know we're safe because Tigger always thought of himself as a guard cat.

The Night Visitor

By Rachel Lister

Around two months ago my sister and I went to stay with our parents, who live in France. They had taken our two cats over with them when they moved around a year ago. While staying there I got used to the cats jumping up on the bed in the middle of the night.

When I returned back to the United Kingdom, my sister came to stay with me at my house for a few days before returning to her home in London. One particular day was very strange indeed and a few things had happened; our salt pot kept turning itself on to the point we had to remove its battery, and we had seen a very peculiar light hovering over the house in front of mine going backward and forward. It was just a really weird day.

That night, I went to bed and my sister slept in our spare bedroom. I awoke in the middle of the night to what felt like a cat jumping onto my bed. (It's one of those things that you recognize, as it sort of lands with a thud and then you feel the paws walking up the bed.) But I didn't have a cat.

I looked down the bed, quite scared at this point, and saw nothing. I was hoping it was perhaps my boyfriend, who may have moved his feet. I tried to get back to sleep.

The following day we went out for lunch and I told my boyfriend and sister about the odd experience I had had and how I thought a cat had jumped onto the bed. My sister went really quiet and then said, "It's funny you should mention that because I had exactly the same thing happen last night, too." Very weird.

Fat and Sassy

by Tom Denney

My cats were named Fat and Sassy. Fat was a twenty-two-pound male and Sassy was a nine-pound female. Sassy was always very playful, but Fat was oppressive, sullen, and very moody. I always hoped that Fat would go first to give Sassy a few years of relief from his moodiness, but that did not happen.

I hated it when Fat would stare Sassy down, and she would have to assume the submissive posture. When I caught this going on, I would clap my hands once and shout his name. That would break things up immediately.

One evening, about a week after Sassy passed away, I was watching television and I saw Fat staring Sassy down again. I started to stand up to do the clap and shout routine, when I realized "Oh, no! She's already gone." Obviously, Fat saw her since he was staring her down, and I saw her very clearly as well.

I had a roommate at the time who said he saw Sassy tearing up and down the stairs like she did a hundred times a day. This was significant because right before her passing she had lost circulation to a back paw, and that was the signal of the beginning of the end.

Fat passed away about a month and a half after Sassy did. I have not seen either one since then. It tore me up terribly to go through the same thing with him that I went through with Sassy, and in such a short time frame. But I know they've survived the transition and are waiting for me on the other side.

The Phantom Kitty

by Athena Sydney

One morning, I awakened at my friends' house to what I thought was their cat, Sam, walking over the duvet on top of me. He approached me, purring loudly. I murmured, "Hi, Sam," then turned and dozed off again. About an hour later I awoke and looked around the room. There was no Sam in sight, and the door was closed. Puzzled by this phenomenon, I sat up and glanced around the room again. Still, there was no cat in sight. Slowly, I rose to my feet and looked under the bed.

"Sammie, are you hiding under there?" I asked. "Come here, kitty."

No cat under the bed either. The cat had been there before; I was certain of it.

After sliding my feet into my slippers, I left the room and stepped into the living room. The room was still deserted, except for Sam, the cat. He stared up at me with his big amber eyes, then he winked at me. I sat down next to him and stroked his black fur, whispering softly to him how pretty he was.

Shortly afterward, my friends came downstairs and I told them about the strange appearance of a cat in my room when the door was closed. Suddenly, one of them grinned, saying; "So you've seen her, too?"

"Her?" I asked, flabbergasted, because Sam was a male cat. I'm sure the amazement was clearly visible on my face.

"Yes," he said. "Our other cat, the one that passed on about six weeks ago. She still haunts the house and enjoys toying with us."

"But I didn't see her," I said. "I just felt a cat walking on my bed, and I heard purring."

"That surely was her," he said with a grin. "She likes to play pranks on an unsuspecting audience. Many times I have walked down the stairs and tripped over her, even though she is gone."

I couldn't believe my ears. What was he trying to tell me—a cat that was refusing to cross over to the other side? And at the same time I knew it was true, because I had felt her around me. I'd heard her purr, which was her way to communicate with the living.

"Are you absolutely certain it was her?" I asked.

"Sure sounds like it," he said, smiling at me. Then, he walked to the bookshelves and picked up a book. "Here, read this book," he said.

I looked at the book cover; it was black, and I read the bright purple letters: *Pet Sematary* by Stephen King.

"What are you trying to tell me?" I asked.

He grinned at me, "I'm sure you'll enjoy the read now that you've experienced the presence of our resident ghost kitty. The book is about a cat that keeps on returning from the dead. In a way it reminds me of our cat." The grin on his face turned into a gentle smile.

I took the book and, with Sam by my side, started to read. And as I read Stephen King's words, I stroked Sam's fur. Every now and again I looked down at him, and he winked up at me, almost as if he were trying to say, "See, I told you everything was going to be okay."

Of course, I had believed in ghosts before. After all, there was one that stood by my side ever since I was twelve years old, protecting me from serious harm. But a phantom cat was something I'd never encountered before.

When I left my friends' house a few days later, I knew this was one vacation I wasn't going to forget. The phantom kitty enriched my life, and I am so thankful for that!

The Ghost Cat of Regester Street

by Amy Lynwander and Melissa Rowell,
Fell's Point Ghost Tours

The Baltimore neighborhood of Fell's Point is one of the oldest in the city. It was spared from destruction by the Great Fire in 1904 and contains many fine examples of Federal Period architecture. Fell's Point was founded in 1730 by a Quaker shipbuilder from Lancaster, England, named William Fell. He envisioned the neighborhood becoming a shipbuilding center. In time his vision came to pass, and many ships, including the famous Baltimore Clipper Ship, were built in this neighborhood. Fell's Point was also home to a large number of privateers. Privateers held "Letters of Marque" for the U.S. government that allowed them to legally seize British ships and any cargo aboard them during the Revolutionary War. Naturally, the British reviled this neighborhood and its inhabitants, and gave it the nickname, "that den of pirates." During the Battle of Baltimore in 1814 the British were specifically trying to reach Fell's Point in order to raze it. They never made it past Fort McHenry and the neighborhood was spared.

All of the people living in Fell's Point during the 1700s, its golden days of shipbuilding, were connected to the maritime industry in some way. There were ship captains, caulkers (including the famous African American abolitionist, Frederick Douglass), tavern owners, ladies of the night, free blacks, and slaves. The rich and poor lived elbow to elbow, with the grand houses of the moneyed adjoining the tiny alley homes of the less prosperous working poor. One of these alley homes is now home to a mysterious feline spirit.

Regester Street is a tiny alley street just one block from the Fell's Point Square, the center of this small village. Its charming tilting homes are crammed together and one can only imagine the lives of the inhabitants packed inside those walls. One building in particular is a way station for lost souls. More than five ghosts, one of whom is the ghost of a gray cat, inhabit the building. The owner of the house has been a resident there for more than fifteen years. Many guests who have visited her have commented on her gray cat.

"I saw your cat in the living room. When I tried to pet it, it hissed and ran away," one guest said.

The owner of the Regester Street house has no pets. As time wore on more and more people told her that they had seen her cat in various rooms of the house. She had no idea why people kept seeing a gray cat in the house. A few years later she was having some contract work done on the basement of the house. The workers were digging up the earth beneath the floor in preparation for installing a new floor. They then uncovered the body of a petrified gray cat, one that appeared to have been dead for quite some time. The animal was desiccated with its skin still on its body—and patches of gray fur were clinging to it! The mystery of the gray ghost cat was solved.

One evening a tour guide for Fell's Point Ghost Tours was standing in front of the house telling the story of the gray cat, among others, when a member of the audience began to heckle her. This woman told the tour guide that there is no way that the cat's fur could have survived such a burial. As the tour group turned to leave Regester Street the woman tripped and fell onto the pavement. She said that a gray cat had just run between her legs. No one else saw the cat.

The Talking Cat

by James Griffiths

I am a spiritualist medium based in Cheshire, England. Over the years I have done readings for many people, and their pets have come through. For the owners these have been lovely heart-warming events knowing that their pets are okay. But on one occasion it was different.

I was working on a project for a company, and I was doing readings and spiritual work only part-time then. One Monday morning we received a phone call from one of the staff saying she would not be in because her cat had taken ill. (To be honest I think it had been run over by a car and the vets were trying to save its life.) She was so devastated that she was prepared to put her job, which she had only been doing for about three weeks, on the line. She had asked if she could have advanced holiday time, and the company was so laid back they said yes. Two weeks later she came back to work and went into her office about 11 a.m., and I decided to go and see her.

I said to her, "I was sad to hear about your cat but as you know I believe in the spirit world, so I know it has gone to a better place." The tears filled up in her eyes, and she said, "I tried everything, James. He just went. He had no fight left."

I asked her to walk with me to the canteen, and as she walked out of her office I looked to the left of the door where a desk was placed. To my amazement on top of the desk was a cat! I stopped and said to this lady, "Do you believe me when I say your cat is okay?" and she said, "Yes and no, James. I want to believe but it's hard." So I had to tell her what was on the desk.

This cat was brown, which to me was unusual. It was quite big as well, twice the size of the average cat. I looked at it and described it to her. The tears again welled up in her eyes and she asked me, "Is he all right now?"

I'm sure this is going to sound strange to everyone who reads this, but the cat replied, "Yes, I am okay." I was completely shocked because as he spoke his mouth moved. (I know you're probably thinking, "What is he on?" But the cat spoke.) He said he loved his spot next to the radiator and he liked the bed that she got for him last week. He also said he was sorry for being so cranky at times. He was also aware of some personal stuff between the lady and her husband. (Well, he was part of the family, so he was bound to know.)

I got the impression from the cat that he was very moody; he did not like certain foods. He was talking to me as though he was a human spirit. I was completely gob smacked.

"I can't believe this," I said to this lady. "The cat is talking." She was a bit confused herself but totally convinced it was her cat, as only he would know about the things in the house, the trouble he had caused in the past, and things he had heard. I know it sounds mad but it's true.

After I stood there talking to the cat, the lady said, "I'm not happy that he has gone (which he had not), but I am happy he is now okay." We became good friends after this, talking about the cat and her life, but the cat never came back like he did that day.

3

HOUNDS AND HAUNTINGS

Shasta

by Toby Longbrake

When I was growing up I thought the greatest hero on earth was Rin Tin Tin. I always wanted a German shepherd, and I felt so lucky when a friend offered me a three-month-old puppy that she couldn't sell. My husband and I took the puppy sight unseen. When we saw her, she scared us because she was so huge. She weighed fifty-five pounds! We took her straight to the vet, and he thought her weight might be close to the record. She was so majestic that we named her Shasta, after Mount Shasta. What a blessing she was to us.

Shortly afterward, my three-year-old grandson, Ryan, came to live with us. Shasta often slept with him and I always knew he was safe with her. He also used to lie beside her and she would strap her legs around him and he would tell her all his troubles. When Ryan wasn't with Shasta, she was with me. She sat by my side while I was on my computer.

When Shasta turned six, I had a really bad feeling that something was wrong with her. I took her to my vet and he ran a complete blood count on her. I also had X-rays done. Nothing was wrong. After I did this twice, my vet told me the only thing wrong with my dog was that she was completely healthy.

About a month later, my husband woke me up and said Shasta was really sick; she was vomiting. I got up and held her and told her I would get her help. I left her on her blanket in the kitchen, took Ryan to school, and went to work. I left work at 8:45 a.m. and returned home to take Shasta to the doctor. She wasn't in the kitchen when I got there. I went to look for her and found she had gone into Ryan's room, and it was there she had died. I was hysterical. I rushed Shasta to the vet to find out what had happened, and he told me her stomach had twisted. There was no test that could have warned us. My grandson was devastated, as were we all.

A couple days went by and I was on the computer. My husband was in the kitchen and Ryan was in his room. I felt Shasta beside me and instinctively reached over to pet her. She rubbed up against me as she always did. And then I remembered she was gone. I let out a scream and ran into the kitchen.

My grandson says he always feels safe in his room because he feels Shasta's presence there. We have seen her in the hall, and we've also seen her shadow in the yard when Ryan was out there.

Our other dog, Kelly, loved Shasta. She sometimes barks at nothing while wagging her tail, and when she does this we feel that Shasta has come back to play with her.

After the initial shock of feeling Shasta rubbing against me, I have found peace with the shadows. I've even talked to her about all my troubles.

Guardian of the Graveyard

by Stacie Savage

I am a lead investigator with IAGhostHunters, a paranormal research team located in Dallas County, Iowa. I would like to share with you the report from a recent investigation in which we encountered our first animal apparition.

This particular investigation took place in an old and very large cemetery in Dallas County, Iowa. It was a very clear night with perfect weather conditions for an investigation, so we used this opportunity to examine a new location. One more interesting fact about this investigation is that it took place on October 17, 2005, which was the occurrence of the lunar full moon cycle. It is a fact that the moon cycles affect our lives in many ways. The gravitational effect of the moon traveling through its cycle around the earth may also be responsible for increases in electromagnetic energy on the earth. This is the type of energy that is believed to be at the root of paranormal activity.

The investigation began around 8 p.m. We started it with a quick walk-through of the northwestern area. The cemetery was quite large with several different areas, so we decided to start recording after covering that section, as we picked up very cold sensations in the western part of the cemetery. We began recording with an EVP recorder, digital camera, and video camera. About twenty minutes into the investigation, we were researching the "cold spots" and taking many photos of that area.

Fellow investigator, Shaun Lewis, and I were extremely amazed when we saw a very dark, shadowy figure peering up from behind a gravestone approximately fifteen feet in front of us. We continued snapping photos and then went on to explore the remainder of the cemetery. All other areas of the grounds seemed to be quiet and warm—a definite temperature change from the western area. We investigated the entire area and found the western area certainly had the feeling of spirits present.

The only activity we encountered around the southeastern area was when trying to capture EVPs. A skunk showed up right under our noses and gave us quite a fright! We thought nothing of this moment, until researching the EVP recordings. After we had the run-in with the skunk, we were laughing and Shaun made a remark to the spirits, "Thanks for the warning!" Then we heard a loud voice on the EVP saying, "Go!"

We then headed back to the southwestern area, where we felt the heavy presence of spirits and Shaun had the strong feeling of someone watching him. He felt it very strongly in front of a particular headstone and requested that I photograph around the stone. (Note: this is in the same area we previously saw the black shadowy apparition.) We took almost ninety digital shots and had video and EVP footage. This investigation lasted around two hours.

After reviewing the photos we were extremely amazed and very pleased for what was intended as a very casual investigation. There were orbs caught in about ninety percent of our photos and we captured the most fascinating animal apparition. It was a rottweiler dog and was caught on the very stone that Shaun had me photograph—truly an amazing find! The dog's ears, glowing eyes, nostrils, tongue, and cheek could clearly be seen coming off of the straight side of the gravestone.

This investigation has truly opened new our eyes and touched our hearts. Never before had we caught such an amazing apparition, let alone an animal apparition. We as a team are now dedicated to broadening our horizons and researching more into animal apparitions. We have gone back to the investigation site to take more photos of the actual gravestone and the family plot that surrounds it. We took photos at the same time of night, from the same angle and additional angles, but were unable to capture this apparition again. This is a great indication that the apparition was not some sort of glare off of the gravestone.

In our research we have found that it is believed that black dog apparitions are sometimes sighted at places where violent crimes have occurred. It is reported that many black dog apparitions are sighted on roads, bridges, doorways, wayside burials, gravesites, and often near water. Much of our research also states that most of the black dog apparitions have the same characteristic of "glowing eyes," as we had seen in our photo.

Some researchers say that common folklore suggests that the black dog apparitions with the "glowing eyes" characteristic actually portrays a bad omen and could be a sign of death to come of the person who sighted it, or one of that person's loved ones. Another folklore about these apparitions states that an evil spirit has been forced to take the form of the dog. Obviously, neither of these speculations has been proven; they are just very common folklore.

Most of our research points to the conclusion that black dog apparitions sighted in graveyards are there to "guard" their owners' site, or that they may just be a common guard for the entire graveyard. Whatever the case may be, this is one sighting that has us intrigued and devoted to learning more about animal apparitions.

The Ghost Dog of Pondtown Creek

by Gerina Dunwich

The frightful apparition of a large white dog haunts the road near a small wooden bridge that crosses Pondtown Creek in Hartford, Alabama. According to local legend, a man was driving on the road when a German shepherd suddenly darted out in front of him. His car hit the dog. But instead of stopping to help the dog, this heartless individual drove off, leaving the poor animal to die from its injuries. It is said that on moonless nights, the dog's ghost wanders the road searching for the driver who took its life. Sometimes it can be heard howling as well.

Duke

by Kelli Driscoll

For years, I wondered if my beloved animals were near after death—if they came to check on us. Sometimes I even wondered if an odd orb in a photo was a soul who came to visit. I recently got my answer.

My husband and I have had Great Danes for years, and we always try to have a rescue Dane as well. Our last rescue was Duke. He was seven when we got him—which is old in Great Dane years.

Duke was sickly when we got him. We learned that he was diabetic, and I began giving him insulin injections twice daily. He neither flinched nor complained. In fact, he thrived! He gained weight, became very playful, and just seemed so happy.

I am not sure what his life was like before, but he lived like a king with us, and he always seemed grateful. He was the sweetest boy, and loved to cuddle. I loved him dearly.

After about three years, it became obvious that his time was really short. During the last month of his life he began to lose bladder control a bit at night. We decided that instead of punishing him by moving him to the kitchen, we would put a great big plastic sheet over his bed and cover it with comforters. He could stay in our room with us (which is where he had been since the day we brought him home) and, if I needed to, I could wash the comforters during the day. It actually worked out well, because the plastic sheet would rustle a bit when he moved at night, and toward the end, I always looked over to check on him.

Finally, early one Saturday morning, Duke awoke and struggled to get outside. More than once, we had to help him stand. As hard as it was, we knew what had to be done. We called the vet and took Duke in. Of course, I was crying and upset, as was my husband.

I have always been with my animals when they were put down. In fact, with Danes, I lay on the floor with them until they are gone; it's just the last gift I can give them. As hard as that is, I could not even imagine them crossing over alone. I am determined that my voice will be the last they hear, and that they will feel my body next to theirs.

We came home and later that day I washed all of Duke's bedding, folded it neatly, and asked my husband to please take the bag outside. It just broke my heart to look at my side of the bed, where Duke slept.

Later that night, we had gotten into bed and were just lying there talking, mostly about the sorrow of the day and when we thought we would be able to bring Duke home. You see, I have all of my animals cremated, and they are here with us. Well, during a lull in the conversation, I distinctly heard Duke's bed rustle. I lay there for a few seconds, very quiet, because at first I did not believe what I had heard! And then my husband said very softly, "Did you hear that? It was Duke's bed. It's okay; he is home now!"

There was nothing else in the room that could have made that sound! And you know, I truly believe that it was Duke just giving us a sign that it was okay; he was home. I truly believe it was his final little "thank-you."

The Ghostly Chemist and His Labrador

by Vikki Anderson

When my husband Jim and I moved into our first home in a quaint lake community in 1980, we were quite surprised to discover that it was haunted.

We had unpacked only the necessary boxes on our first night. There were the normal new house noises that one would expect. After detecting what they were, we continued unpacking and catching a snack before going to bed.

Both Jim and I heard the croaking of the frogs from the lake a hundred feet away. We were lulled to sleep by the lovely and soothing sound of a waterfall that we faintly heard in the distance, as well as by the chirping of crickets to each other trying to find a mate. Both of us had felt blessed by getting this lovely home in this lake community. This would be the house of our dreams, we thought.

The very first night was an odd one to say the least. We had one cat, Phraddy Cat, who loved to go to the toilet seat and play with it. He would throw it up in the air with his paws and look at it in amazement when it fell back down with a loud crash. The noise was annoying, so I got out of bed to shoo the cat away from the bathroom only to find him fast asleep on the living room sofa. That was odd, I thought. I went back to bed and didn't say anything about it.

Then we were both startled to hear boxes falling in our bedroom. We were sleeping in the dining room at the time since it was the only room that did not have boxes stacked floor to ceiling. This happened many times throughout the night, but being in the metaphysical field, I assured my husband that if these were indeed spirits and they wanted to hurt us, we would have been hurt by now. I fell deeply asleep, but my husband didn't get a good night's sleep for several weeks.

The days went on and on and the noises kept up each evening as we got ready for bed and throughout the night. It unnerved my husband, a convert to believing in spirits, but after a while I just attributed it to a soul or two who didn't follow the light and were trapped in our house. I felt sorry for them and had planned to burn white sage and say prayers to put them at rest and send them to the astral plane.

But with new houses, there is always something to do, and before I had a chance to get to the local New Age shop to buy sage, I saw a ghost. One day as I was cleaning the kitchen, I caught a glimpse of a large black dog running past me and into the living room. I was tired, so I didn't think much of it. But later that day when I was vacuuming the living room, I saw the same dog run into the bedroom we hadn't yet unpacked. Then I heard more boxes fall over. The mystery was solved.

That evening, as we were eating dinner on the enclosed back porch, I glanced out of the glass door and saw a man in a white suit looking in at us. I casually told my husband and he asked, "What should we do?"

"Nothing; we really can't do anything now, just eat."

That night, more boxes were knocked over, and we heard the scraping of tools on the concrete basement floor. When we looked in the basement, however, nothing was there. More boxes in the attic and the bedroom were knocked over. It was a bizarre cycle that I desperately wanted to break.

Throughout the following weeks, I repeatedly saw the gentleman in the white suit outside; he never came into my home. I continuously heard the knocking down of boxes and the toilet seat cover being played with.

Finally, I contacted the Realtor who sold us the house, who incidentally was the daughter of the couple who had lived in the house prior to our moving in. I asked her, "Did you have a dog?"

She told me that the family dog was a beautiful black Lab that had run off when her father died. They never knew what happened to it.

I also asked if her father wore white suits. She looked at me in a perplexed manner and said, "Well, he was a chemist and always had to wear his white lab coat. Why, did you see him?"

Now, if my father had passed on, I don't think I would ask if someone had seen him. So did she know her father's spirit was bound to the house?

I finally had time to buy the white sage and burned it throughout the house, attic, basement, garage, and yard. I did this twice during one day and said prayers to the Goddess and the universe asking that the souls who were trapped inside and outside of my home would be guided to the light and move on with their incarnation to the astral plane. I did this in a loving and compassionate manner.

I also went throughout the house and in the yard and said to the beings that were there, "You are not supposed to be here anymore. Look toward the light. Take your dog and move on. You are supposed to be learning about your next incarnation. You cannot stay earthbound any longer. God bless."

Amazingly enough, from that time on, we have had no other visitors living with us—except for the human kind that I personally invited in—and have been enjoying our home spirit-free ever since.

The Bloodstained Basement

by E. G. Gruebner

The house on Essex Street seemed perfect. It was close to the school where I worked, and it had a large fenced-in yard for my miniature collie, Ruby. But best of all, the monthly rent was considerably lower than other places in the area.

Immediately after moving into the house I noticed a change in Ruby's behavior. She acted nervous and would often hide under my bed, trembling and refusing to come to me when I'd call her name. I figured she just needed some time to adjust to the new surroundings, even though we had moved several times in the past and she never reacted in such a strange way.

One night, around ten o'clock, I awoke to whimpering and scratching sounds coming from the kitchen. I went to investigate and found Ruby clawing at the door leading to the basement.

"What's the matter, girl?" I asked. "Is there something down in the basement?"

Ruby let out a couple small yelps and then put her nose to the bottom of the door as if she were picking up a scent.

I decided to open the door and let the dog go down and explore the basement. As I unlocked the door and started turning the knob, Ruby started whining loudly and pacing back and forth. I had never seen her act so disturbed about anything before and I wasn't quite sure what to make of her peculiar behavior.

I opened the door and, before I even had a chance to switch on the basement light, Ruby bolted down the stairs as if chasing after something. Within a matter of seconds she had disappeared into the dank and musty darkness below. Almost immediately she began growling.

I switched on the light and from the top of the stairs I could see Ruby. Her attention was clearly focused on something on the floor. I went downstairs and upon closer inspection it turned out to be a faded brown stain resembling half a butterfly.

The only other time I had been in the basement was when the landlady showed me around the house, but I didn't recall seeing any stain on the floor then. Perhaps I was just too excited about the house to notice.

A few days later I went down to the basement to do some laundry and Ruby followed me. I saw her stop dead in her tracks as soon as she got near the stain. She let out a low growl and began to slowly back up. She then started barking wildly and darting back and forth. I took her upstairs and she finally calmed down.

That weekend I went downstairs with a scrub brush and some scouring powder and attempted to remove the stain from the floor. I scrubbed and scrubbed, and even tried different cleansers, but nothing would take the stain out. I gave up and started up the stairs when all of a sudden something shadowy darted past me. Startled and a bit spooked, I looked around but there was nothing there. I hurried upstairs and quickly locked the basement door behind me.

The following day when I arrived home from school I was startled to find the basement door wide open. It had been locked when I left the house that morning. I called to Ruby but she did not answer. The house felt icy cold and the eerie silence became overwhelming. Fearing that someone had broken in to the house while I was at work, I quietly tiptoed out through the backdoor and then ran to a neighbor's house where I phoned the police.

Within a few minutes they arrived on the scene and, with their guns drawn, checked out my house from top to bottom. They found no signs of a forced entry and nothing seemed to be missing. I asked one of the officers if they had seen my dog and he told me they had. She was down in the basement hiding behind the oil tank.

After the police left, I phoned my landlady about having the locks changed. I also asked her about the stain on the basement floor. What she told me made the hairs on my arms stand up.

Her grandfather lived in the house in the 1930s and kept a Doberman as a watchdog and a family pet. One day his dog went into a rage and attacked one of his children while they were playing in the yard. He took the dog down to the basement, chained it to a pipe, and then gave it a severe beating with a wooden leg from an old chair. The following day when he went back down into the basement he found the dog was dead. It was curled up and in a pool of blood, which left a stain on the floor.

After hearing that, I told my landlady about Ruby's strange behavior and said, "This is probably going to sound crazy to you, but I'm starting to think the ghost of that Doberman is haunting the basement."

She surprised me by saying she didn't think it was crazy at all. In fact, she said her grandfather eventually became convinced that the dead dog's spirit wanted revenge, and he avoided the basement at all costs! She also told me that when she and her brother and sister were growing up in the house, they, too, had seen the fleeting shadow of a dog in the basement and would sometimes even hear a dog panting or growling.

One day her brother's friend from school was over playing hide-and-seek with them and claimed to have been chased up the basement stairs by a black dog that disappeared when it reached the top step. However, she wasn't sure if the story was true or if the boy had just made it up in order to scare her and her sister.

After our enlightening conversation, I returned to the basement and drew a small circle around the bloodstain with a piece of white chalk. I sprinkled some salt and sage inside the circle, covered it with a small braided rug, and prayed for the dog's restless spirit to find peace.

I had never done anything ritualistic like that before but it just felt like the correct thing to do at the time and under the circumstances. It seemed to have a positive effect because during the remaining three years that Ruby and I lived in that house, her behavior was normal and there were no further incidents in the bloodstained basement.

Rebel

by Suzy Johnson

My mom was working as a home health aide in 1980, and she was particularly fond of one family in her care. When this family's dog gave birth, my mom was given one of the puppies—a little black schnauzer I named Rebel.

Rebel soon became my dog, I guess because I gave him most of the attention. We were always together. Sometimes when Rebel and I sat in the living room and watched TV, I noticed Rebel's attention on something in the room that I couldn't see. Apparently, someone or something was walking around the room and Rebel was focusing on them, his head moving in slow, steady motion back and forth. He did this almost daily.

In March 1986 I got married and moved a few miles away, and Rebel was left to live with my mom. I thought she would need a companion and Rebel was the perfect choice. He would always alert us when someone we couldn't see was in the room.

Around 1995 my mom told me that Rebel had a lot of tumors in his chest area. This broke my heart because I knew his days were numbered. He had trouble breathing, and walking down the hall left him winded. So I did the only humane thing I could and took him to the vet to be gently put out of his misery. I stayed with him the whole time and when the end was near I whispered in his ear, "Please come back to us Rebel, you can do it." Heartbroken, I left the vet's office and brought Rebel's body home to be buried in the backyard under Mom's bedroom window. The house seemed really empty without him. He was such a sweet dog.

One day, a few months later, I went to mom's house to see her but she wasn't home. I had a key, so I let myself in and sat in the living room for a while. I wasn't thinking about anything in particular when I just happened to look up through the living room doorway into the dining room and I saw Rebel run past. He had so much energy as he ran past; it was obvious he was having fun doing something he couldn't have done in his last few months of life. And it gave me great comfort knowing he had come home.

I now own my mom's house and Rebel's visits are few and far between. But last year a family member visited and told us he "saw something solid black and low to the floor" run down the hallway toward my mom's old bedroom. I asked him what he thought it was and he said, "I don't know what it was, but I know I saw something." I just grinned because I knew Rebel was paying us another visit.

A Visitation from Vanna

by Kathleen Cunzeman

We had recently got a puppy to "replace" our fourteen-year-old gold Lab, Vanna, who passed a few months before. The new dog is also gold colored. At thirty-five-pounds, she is much smaller than Vanna, about half of her size. We also have a sixty-five-pound black Lab.

My husband's mother and stepfather were visiting from Florida. We live in Maryland and it had probably been six years since they last came to our house. Anyway, there was much excitement when they arrived. The puppy, which is very friendly, was jumping up and down at the door and we were doing our best to contain her. The black Lab, of course, was also waiting at the door to greet them, but just wagging his tail in his laid-back way.

They finally made it into the living room, and we stopped and talked there for a few minutes. They wanted to see the family room on the lower level of our tri-level house that we had remodeled last year, so I took them downstairs. My husband took the puppy upstairs, put a leash on her, and brought her back downstairs.

While we were down there, my father-in-law asked me, "When did you get the third dog?"

I said, "What do you mean, Bob, by the third dog? Our other dog died in November, right before my father. We got the puppy in January."

My mother-in-law said, "Yes, Bob, I know you remember me telling you the dog died and how upset they were over it."

And he said again, "Well, there are three dogs in this house. I clearly saw three dogs greet us at the door and three dogs standing in the living room when we were talking."

I was really curious at this point and asked him what the other dog looked like. He said it was a large, gold dog. I pointed down at the puppy and my black Lab and asked, "Bob, are you sure you saw another dog, because we only have two dogs."

He got a little annoyed with me at this point and said, "I know what I saw and I am positive there were three dogs in the living room."

Bob is a very practical and intelligent man, and my mother-in-law later told me that in the car all the way to the restaurant he insisted that we had three dogs. He was convinced we were lying for some reason about only having two dogs because he was so adamant about three greeting him.

I believe the third dog he saw must have been Vanna in spirit. I have seen her, too, at times, and she probably just dropped by because of my in-laws' special visit to our home.

Buttons and the Blue Gingham Bow

by Lisa Armstrong

One of the first things my parents deemed necessary was to fulfill a child's version of the American dream . . . to own and care for a pet of our own. In May of 1972 we adopted a beautiful little black Lab/mix puppy that my brother and I named Buttons. I was five years old at the time, and we had just moved into our first house in Marietta, Pennsylvania. Within a month, my brother and I grew very close to this little package of love.

The remnants of Hurricane Agnes came to visit and play havoc on our little riverside town that June. The storm may not have had the horrible winds of a Category 5 hurricane, but its size, which covered around a thousand miles, was catastrophic as far as the rain went. So, my family was forced to evacuate our newly moved into home, and leave our precious little Buttons behind.

I remember my fear and anger for having to leave Buttons behind, but Dad told us she would be fine, and that the water would reach our basement only. If by some nightmare the water rose higher, he said he would get there in time to take her somewhere safe.

Like he said, we got four feet of water in our basement. It never reached the upstairs. He went to the house a few times a day to feed

Buttons and tie her to the balcony so she could get fresh air. One day, he went back to check on her, and to his horror she was not there. I thought for sure she ventured into the murky water of the Susquehanna and drowned. I cried my heart out and prayed for God to keep her safe and let us find her. Praise God, someone did find that little vagabond wandering Market Street. And through word of mouth, we were reunited. This made my bond with this special dog even stronger.

As I grew up, I found myself confiding my deepest, darkest secrets to her as only an eight-year-old could do. I remember holding her close when she ran to greet me every day after school. I was very overweight and more often that not, other students chanted harsh names at me during the school day. I would hold it inside all day so they couldn't see how much they hurt me with their cruel words. But when I got home, I would hold Buttons tight and press my chubby face against her velvet coat and cry my little heart out. She always seemed to understand and licked my tears away.

In 1982, I was in the tenth grade and Buttons was ten years old. My family decided to move to a neighboring county. It was the middle of the school year and I was terrified to move to a new home and new school. I worried about Buttons, too. She only knew this house and this town. Buttons did okay with the move but her disposition changed and I guess, like a human, the stress of it all made her age.

By the following January, her health was failing. When she started having accidents, she would look at us with those big pitiful brown eyes. You could see the shame and I felt so sorry for her. Dad would get angry, thinking Buttons was getting too lazy to go outside.

I remember comforting her. It was my pleasure to return the

kindness she always showed me. She would lay her head on my lap and I would pet that wonderful dog until she fell asleep.

My brother tied a blue gingham bow to her collar. It seemed to make her feel pretty, and she liked the fuss we made over her. When her accidents continued, we took her to the vet and Buttons was diagnosed with diabetes. We had to put her down.

I was heartbroken. My mom was worried about me and told me she was going to take me to a psychiatrist if I didn't soon snap out of it. But I lost my best friend. I couldn't eat or sleep. I just felt so lost. My brother wanted the bow to remember her by, but it had disappeared. We looked everywhere for it but to no avail.

A few months later, still very depressed, I walked around our huge backyard just thinking of every memory of Buttons that I could. I walked over to the far side of our yard where it met up with an overgrown lot and an adjoining stream.

I thought I heard something walking in the weeds, swishing and crunching as it made its way toward me. I stopped and stood very still, thinking maybe it was a rabbit. I walked along the weeds toward the noise. I stopped once more and found myself standing there watching the high, dead weeds sway a bit as my "rabbit" made its way toward me.

As it got close enough for me to see down into the base of the weeds where the movement was occurring, I was shocked to see nothing there. I wondered if it was a ghost. Still, I wasn't afraid. I stood very still as the movement inched closer and closer, stopping when it reached the edge of the weeds right in front of me. Then it was still. Nothing.

I looked down at my feet. There, lying between them was that little gingham bow that belonged to Buttons. She wanted me to know she was okay. It was her way of telling me she would always be with me in one form or another. Despite a wet and windy winter the bow was clean and showed no signs of distress. I picked it up and held it close to my heart and whispered to the weeds, "Thank you, Buttons, I will always love you, too."

After that experience I slowly started to come out of my depression. We even got another dog. Her name was—Bow, of course.

The Ballechin House Hauntings

by Gerina Dunwich

Built in Perthshire, Scotland, in 1806, the Highland mansion known as the Ballechin House is believed by many to be haunted by supernatural dogs and human ghosts.

Major Robert Steuart inherited the estate from his father in 1834 and lived there for more than a quarter-century with only his dogs for company. Steuart was a believer in reincarnation and transmigration (the passing of the soul into another body), but it was a certain odd request that earned him the reputation of an eccentric among the local townsfolk. He wished that after taking his final breath, his disembodied spirit would return from the dead and live on within the body of his favorite dog, a black spaniel.

Steuart died in 1876, leaving the mansion to his sister's son John and his family. John knew well of the Major's final wish but found the very idea of his uncle's spirit taking up residence within the physical body of one of his dogs so abominable that he had every one of the animals on the estate put to death.

Afterward, strange and inexplicable occurrences began to take place in the house. Sounds like rapping, violent knockings, footsteps, explosions, and quarreling voices filled the air and an icy chill gripped the house.

John's wife reported smelling the unmistakable odor of dogs when alone in the Major's study and even claimed to have felt an invisible canine push against her when there were no animals in the house.

In 1892 a Jesuit priest, while spending two nights as a guest at Ballechin House, said he heard loud rapping and unexplained screams and animal-like sounds. The unnerving experience led him to the conclusion that the place was haunted.

The mansion was later rented out to a group of paranormal investigators, who invited thirty-five unsuspecting guests to stay at Ballechin House while the investigators conducted an experiment in the unknown. Some of the guests reported seeing the apparition of a black spaniel and hearing the tail of a ghostly dog hitting against the doors. One female guest claimed to have witnessed a pair of disembodied dog's paws materialize on the nightstand table in her bedroom and then fade from sight. In addition to the spectral canines, a number of guests encountered ghosts of the human variety, including one of a weeping woman believed to have been a nun. A mysterious detached hand holding a crucifix and floating in the air was also seen.

In the year 1899, despite strong opposition from the Steuart family, the entire account of the ghost hunters' experiment was published in a book called *The Alleged Haunting of B-House*.

Goldie

by Christopher Kypta

During the summer, my mornings have a certain ritual order to them. I walk down my driveway in the pre-dawn and sit at the mailbox waiting for the sun. It's the most peaceful part of my day. The skies are still a dark blue and the dew is settling on the grass as I sit and watch and listen. The sound of first birdsong comes and the sky lightens in the east.

The sun, still under the horizon, lights the bottom of clouds as they wisp through the sky in an array of scarlet, purple, and gold. Watching the clouds float across the sky, I find it easy to imagine that I am alone atop some mountain in the Far East rather than sitting by my mailbox in the suburbs of Atlanta. Occasionally, however, the lights of a car remind me all too well that Atlanta is not far away and the city is already beckoning its early workers.

It is never too hard to return to the contemplative state I find in watching the dawn come once a car has passed and its taillights fade into the distance, but sometimes there are other visitors as well. My neighbor's golden retriever, Goldie, is always out early in the morning taking her stroll around the block. I can hear her coming down the hill, tags dangling and nails clicking against the asphalt. I'll turn to look up the hill and her tail will wag as she sees me, and sometimes she will come and sit beside me as if she, too, is watching the sunrise.

But one quiet summer morning, no different from the others, something unusual happened. The clouds lolled through the July morning sky as always and the early bird workers headed down the road. Goldie came down the road, too, but that day she surprised me. When I looked up the hill and saw her trotting down the road, I realized I couldn't hear her tags jingling or her nails clicking. I waited for her to come and sit beside me, but she trotted across her yard as if my neighbor were calling her.

Oh well, I thought, and looked away. It was several moments before I remembered that Goldie had died the day before. She had been lying in her driveway when my neighbor backed over her in his car. He took her to the vet, but there was nothing that could be done.

It was then that I realized I had seen a ghost, that I was in the middle of a paranormal experience. I always thought that if I were to see a ghost I would panic, but at that moment I felt calm and the morning seemed very still. I looked across my neighbor's yard.

Goldie was still there, making her way deliberately across the yard to where the driveway snaked around toward the back of the house. As she walked, there was no jingling sound from her dog tags. Goldie walked in silence.

Watching Goldie walk across her yard was almost like looking at a silent movie of a dog. There was no sound, but there was also something odd about how she looked that was so subtle anyone unaware that she was a ghost would have missed. Goldie seemed to be two-dimensional, almost an outline of a dog filled in with golden color. She had reached the driveway now and walked across the asphalt without a single click of her nails and then was gone around the corner of the house.

I got up from the mailbox and went inside. I did not wish to see the sun rise that day, nor for many days to come. But eventually I did return to my perch beside the mailbox. The first time I was very nervous and each bird chirp made me jump as I sat and waited, wondering what I would do if I were to hear the jingling of Goldie's collar coming down the hill or catch a blur of golden color out of the corner of my eye. But nothing happened. The sun rose as it always had and the clouds turned purple, gold, and crimson in the morning sky. No apparition of a dog ever came down the hill again nor took a morning walk around the block. It happened only once. Goldie was run over, taken to the vet's, and put to sleep. Then she came home.

The Dumb Supper

by Kelly Spangler

On October 28, 2004, I was attending what is called a Dumb Supper in Salem, Massachusetts. This is a dinner to honor the dead and the death of loved ones passed over.

As I sat in silence eating my dinner, I had tears in my eyes because I sensed many spirits around us. I suddenly felt the urge to reach down and pet something. I felt a pressure on my leg as if some animal was looking for a bit of comfort. I then got a glimpse of a dog staring straight up at me while resting its head on my leg. It was the spirit of my brother's deceased dog, Cocoa, and this is what she used to do to everyone when she was alive. I was petting her as if she were really there.

After the dinner a friend who was sitting next to me asked, "Why did I have the strong feeling that I needed to throw down food to the floor next to me and you?" This confirmed to me that what I experienced had actually happened.

I started to cry and said, "Because Cocoa was there!"

Ghost of the Angry Dog

by Rosemarie V.

When I was only two years old my mother passed away and my father remarried and left us to live with my maternal grandparents, who lived with my uncle and his family in Mexico. I grew up very poor and was never given anything on birthdays or holidays. But on my twelfth birthday one of our relatives gave me a dog.

My grandfather was a very old-fashioned and strict man, so when I brought the dog home he refused to let me keep it. He said that we didn't have the money to feed ourselves, let alone a dog. But, by this time I was already working, so I convinced him to let me keep it.

I only had my dog for about two months, but during that time we had become the best of friends. I had no other friends or siblings around. All my siblings were older and married.

My oldest cousin, Francisco, who was about ten at the time, hated me very much. I think I felt the same way about him because we were jealous of each other. One day when I came home from work he was standing at the doorway with an evil look on his face and laughing in a most sinister way. He bragged to me that I no longer had a dog. I asked him why he was saying this and he told me that my grandfather had killed it. He said the dog had gotten rabies and had foam coming from his mouth.

Very upset, I went directly to my grandfather. I asked him about this and he told me to go to my room because he didn't want to talk about it. I locked myself in my room and I wouldn't come

110

out or eat for days. My grandmother tried to console me by telling me that my dog was in a better place.

On the fourth day after my dog's death, about five o'clock in the morning, I was lying in bed with my eyes closed when I heard a noise coming from the exposed beams of the ceiling. I immediately felt something jump directly onto my stomach. I opened my eyes and saw my dog. I was so happy to see him. I thanked him for returning to me and told him that it had all been a misunderstanding. My grandfather must have thought he killed him, but my dog was only wounded.

But as I got closer to him to hug and kiss him, I saw that his eyes were very different. They were evil looking as if he had fire in them. He opened his mouth and he had big fangs. I started praying out loud and as soon as I said the word *God*, the dog snarled at me, showing his fangs once again, and then jumped back onto the ceiling beams and disappeared.

I ran to my grandmother's room, but she had already left for church. When she returned I told her about what happened and she was surprised. She said that it had probably happened because I was mad at them and the devil had come to scare me. I didn't believe this so I confronted my cousin. He laughed at me and told me that the dog had bit him, but only after he had pulled really hard on his tail and hurt him. He then had told my grandfather that the dog bit him, and my grandfather killed the dog by stabbing it.

Francisco took me to the hills about a quarter-mile away from my house to prove to me that the dog was dead. He started digging, and sure enough there was my dog as dead as could be. I was so heartbroken.

I never understood why my dog came back to me in such an evil way.

The Scratching on the Bedroom Door

by Lonnie E. Scott

I received a rat terrier puppy when I was thirteen years old, and my family named him Pokey. That dog was the most wonderful friend and companion any young boy could have. He so loved us that he hung on to life through a few bouts of illness that should have killed him. He finally passed on from this world in the winter of 2003.

Three nights after Pokey's departure, I was awakened by a scratching on my bedroom door. I was extremely tired and never thought twice about getting out of bed to let Pokey in so he could sleep with me. I opened the door and watched his tail wagging in excitement as we climbed into bed and went to sleep. It never occurred to me that this shouldn't be happening until the following morning when I realized what had occurred. My heart broke again.

I didn't tell anyone else in the house what had happened until one by one they revealed that they were all awakened by scratching at their doors and also got up to let Pokey in. I knew it wasn't my imagination or a dream after hearing their tales. I knew Pokey was still with us.

I only wish I could scratch his ears again. But I know one day I will.

The Barking of the Phantom Hounds

by Gerina Dunwich

In the book, *Ghostly American Places: A Ghostly Guide to America's Most Fascinating Haunted Landmarks*, one of the places mentioned is a movie theater located on Cliff Gookin Boulevard on the outskirts of Tupelo, Mississippi. Various people who worked there have reported seeing heavy curtains moving by themselves when there were no breezes and hearing strange sounds such as unexplained footsteps, laughter, and mumbling voices.

One night, while cleaning the theater with her sister, the manager's wife went into the projection room and opened the door to a closet containing brooms and a utility sink. She suddenly heard what sounded like "seven or eight dogs barking" despite there being no dogs in the room. When she shut the door, the barking ceased. When she re-opened it, the sound started up again. This curious happening, which occurred only the one time, defies explanation.

Sarge

by Karen Wood

We had a Lhasa apso named Sergeant Bilko, but called him Sarge for short. He used to lay downstairs until we all got ready for bed and then he would run up the stairs as fast as he could, slide around the corner, and run through the kitchen into my bedroom. We could hear his nails clicking as he ran on the tile in the kitchen. He used to come to the foot of my bed and pull part of the bedspread down to make himself a bed to lie down on. This was a nightly routine with him.

After my divorce, I dated and eventually lived with a guy I had gone to school with. Sarge, who wasn't exactly a friendly dog, didn't like him. After some time my boyfriend let the dog loose outside (or so he said) and we never saw him again. Sarge was about ten years old or so at the time, and was already losing his adult teeth. I figured that if he did just run off, he must have left to die. I had heard dogs do that sometimes.

It was about a year after we last saw Sarge when I heard his nails clicking on the tiles in the kitchen. I then heard him running up the stairs and felt him tug the bedspread, pulling it down from my shoulders to make his bed. I hollered at him to knock it off like I usually did before I realized he couldn't be there. I sat up and looked just to be sure. Of course he wasn't there.

I wasn't asleep or dreaming when this happened. In fact, I had just turned off the lights and gotten situated in bed when I heard him.

I only heard Sarge that one time, and the bedspread never again tugged off of me either. Sometimes I wished I hadn't scolded him that one last time; maybe he would have stuck around.

One Last Good-bye

by Suzanne Smith

When my husband and I were younger, our pets were our kids. We had a wonderful raccoon named Cosmo, and a large Old English sheepdog named Snuffy.

Snuffy was our furry son. He went everywhere with us—to the races, to Big Sur to play on the beach, and even to work with me. Everyone loved this big fluff ball. He was a great dog.

His favorite day was Sunday. He would wait for the first sound of us stirring in the bedroom and make a beeline to leap on the bed, where he would be promptly tickled and scratched into doggy nirvana.

As Snuffy aged, we were saddened to find that he had cancer. He didn't seem to be in pain, but he slowed down and slept most of his days away. We waited to see what the vet could do, but before he could take action, Snuffy passed away in his sleep (on a Monday afternoon). We buried him in his favorite spot in the yard and mourned him as if he were our child.

That week the house was so empty.

The following Sunday morning broke clear and crisp. We lay in bed quietly; I'm sure we were both thinking about Snuffy. Suddenly, as my husband and I lay there, we were startled to feel the bed shake as if our big dog had just jumped into his favorite spot once more. We sat straight up and looked at each other. We checked to see if there had been any earthquakes, but none were reported.

Between the laughter and tears we shed that morning, we truly felt that our pal had sent us a message from beyond. I like to think it was Snuffy's way of saying one last good-bye.

Tyson

by Michelle Morgan

Tyson came into my life five years ago as part of my new marriage. Although quite intimidating to look at, this 130-pound rottweiler didn't take long in winning the hearts of my children and me. We gave in to his demands for toast and jelly in the mornings when we were rushing to work and school, and we learned to tolerate being followed about our tiny old house by our oversized "shadow."

We often laughed when people hesitated when they first met Tyson, knowing he was most likely more afraid of them than they were of him. He *did* have a very vicious growl that he saved for strangers but this often emanated from him while hiding behind a door. The only time Tyson seemed overly protective was if I was sleeping and someone came up the stairway that led to our bedroom. He often posted himself right in front of my bedroom door as though he were standing guard until he decided it was safe for him to retreat for the rest of the night into our room.

Tyson would stay close by me while I worked in the house. If I spent too long ignoring him while working on the computer, he came over and knocked my hands off the keys with his head and rested his head in my lap. He never quite figured out that his hulking size didn't make for a good lapdog, and if I attempted to watch TV or read, eventually he tried to crawl in my lap. I attempted to push him off and usually give up when he turned his sad, big brown eyes on me with "that look."

I had to admit I loved him as much as he loved me. He often tried to sneak up on our bed after we fell asleep to nuzzle in next to me. Tyson was content just to be as close as he could to us at all times. I tripped over him many times on my way up the hall in the middle of the night. With his large size, it was hard not to stumble over him at least once a day in our narrow hall leading to the bedrooms. The inconvenience and the stubbed toes were all worth the unconditional love we found in this gentle giant.

As the years went by, Tyson became nearly completely crippled with arthritis. In July of 2005, at the age of thirteen, Tyson fell down the stairs and we couldn't get him to walk. My husband and son carried him in on a blanket and we nursed him all day. When there was no change, we took him to the vet. We had put off the trip there earlier because we all knew this was the end for our beloved friend.

After examining him, the vet said his hips had deteriorated so badly there was nothing left and little hope for any sort of recovery at his age. My husband, son, and daughter all gathered there in the reception room where they brought me the papers to sign to put Tyson to sleep.

I stood with the pen poised, putting off writing my signature that would seal his fate. A little girl who had two very rambunctious terriers with her was standing nearby and asked, "Where is your dog?" I found it difficult to answer her as I felt the lump forming in my throat. Her father realized what was happening and hurried her to a seat across the lobby with her new pups. I stared back at the release form that would allow the vet to put my darling Tyson out of his pain and felt like a traitor. I thought, How could we let him die? A voice in my head also questioned, How can we let him suffer? Tears spilling, I took a deep breath and signed the papers with the stipulation that we all be allowed to see him for a moment alone before he was put down.

I remember going in that room where he was lying and thinking about how much he hated going to the vet. Unlike the other trips he would often take in my van, he would get anxious on the ride to the vet and start carrying on in the car as if he intuitively knew where we were heading. Yet that day, he only lifted his head once and looked at me with resignation. I think he realized his time had come. I looked down on my dear friend lying on the gurney and I realized he looked as weak and helpless as a newborn pup. He was just a shell of what he had once been. I cupped his head in my hands and told him there wasn't going to be any more pain for him and that we loved him very much. I told him that there would be people there in heaven who would watch over him till we were together again. He put his paw on my face and licked at my tears. Even in his weakened state, he was still trying to console and protect me.

My daughter, Jesselyn, and my twenty-year-old son, JJ, were both in tears as they said their good-byes. My husband's shoulders were slumped and tears filled his eyes as he watched and reluctantly came over to bid farewell to Tyson. Once we left the room, a nurse almost immediately came back out to tell me that Tyson had passed. She brought me his leather collar, which I held all the way home.

My heart broke when we arrived home and found our other dog, Chloe, had firmly planted herself in the window looking for Tyson, who had been her surrogate father since the day she arrived in our home as a pup. She cried and paced through the house for several days looking for him and not understanding. The hardest part came when my youngest son, Brett, who adored Tyson most of all, came home from a visit with his dad and we had to break the news to him. Each of us felt an emptiness in our home that nothing could fill. He was as much a part of our family as any person could be and we mourned our loss.

About one month later I awoke in the middle of the night and headed down the hall to the bathroom. Blurry-eyed from sleep, I brushed against the large body I often found there and instinctively whispered, "Tyson, move!" I heard him shift out of the way and give one of his trademark "chuffs," indicating he was disturbed from a nice dream, and I continued on to the bathroom down the hall. Once I reached the bathroom I was fully awake and realized I couldn't have bumped into Tyson. Tyson was gone. I checked for our other dog, Chloe, but she was lying in bed with Brett with the door closed. I was unnerved by the experience and I decided not to mention it for obvious reasons. The following night, my husband said he could have sworn he saw Tyson in the hall. I looked at him and laughed, deciding not to mention what happened just yet.

Over the course of the next few weeks, we saw, heard, or brushed against what we thought was Tyson while in the upstairs hallway. Had he come back to watch over us as we slept as he often did in his life? We may never know the answer, but we have gained great comfort from the thought that even in death, he had not forgotten us.

The Breakfast Companion

by Sheila Hrabal

It all started when I was seventeen and decided I was old enough to move out on my own. My dad knew I was feeling my way around the world and that I felt pretty independent. But one day I told him that I was going on the road to "find myself" with my latest boyfriend who was also seventeen. It was 1976; everybody was doing it and having a blast! And, besides, it wasn't like we were hitchhiking; we were taking our 1970 Cutlass Supreme.

We left our hometown in September that year and hit the open road. Being a teenager, I thought I was all grown up and didn't really need to ever call home while I was away. But I guess my dad had different ideas; after all, to him I was still his "little girl." After I had been out of town for about two months, he started to wonder whether or not I was okay. He began losing sleep, finding it difficult to eat, and becoming irritable whenever someone mentioned my name—all because he was worried.

One day as he was trying to eat breakfast before going to work, he thought he saw something out of the corner of his eye. He glanced over his right shoulder, but saw nothing. He dismissed it as nerves and went on to work that day. A few days later, he felt like he was being watched; again, he was in the kitchen at the breakfast table. He turned to get a better look, but nothing was there. This kept happening for about two more weeks. After a month or so had passed, he got an idea—he would not turn his head when he felt this strange "presence"; he would just move his eyes in the direction where he thought this thing was sitting.

120

He tried this a few times, but whatever it was seemed to know when he was about to look and disappeared into thin air! Eventually, he was able to catch a glimpse of it, and it was a big white dog. The dog was calmly sitting on the floor by the canned goods cabinet, staring back at him, but not moving. After he had seen this dog out of the corner of his eye for a few weeks, he decided to try staring at it head-on. So one day, he steeled his nerves when he felt the dog in the room, turned his head, and looked directly at it. The dog didn't disappear this time until he got up to finish getting ready for work.

Every day from then on, he had his breakfast with this dog. After a while, this dog began to be a comfort to him, but he didn't know why. As the months flew by, I was out having fun seeing the sights of America, without a care in the world. By July of the next year, near my birthday, my boyfriend and I decided we had had enough fun and were finally ready to rejoin the working class and settle down. I called my dad and told him we were coming home.

Shortly after I returned, my dad noticed that the dog started missing breakfast with him. As time passed, the dog disappeared altogether, never to be seen again. Years later, my father told me about this dog and how it had helped him come to terms with my being gone.

As a family, we had never had a dog, but several years after my dad passed away, I came across a white pit bull puppy. She was very loving and playful, and I took her into my home. She goes everywhere with me, and I can't help wondering if he sent her to me to help me get on with my life without him.

Nickalos

by Jakette Foskey

When I first met my husband, Mark, he had a dog that was named Nickalos. He was a mixed breed, mostly rottie. Nick (as we called him) lived at my husband's mother's house when we first got married and was loved by the whole family. He was a great dog. He loved children and would keep a watchful eye on the kids to keep them safe from a nearby lake where we live in Florida.

My husband and I got a home and were able to move Nick in with us. That was a happy time. We loved him, and with my husband working nights, he made me feel safe. But Nick was more afraid of thunderstorms than I was, and it was not unusual to wake up in the middle of the night during a storm and hear him come through the cat door—all ninety pounds of him!

He also greeted visitors that way. He stayed on the back porch or in the garage most of the time, and when he heard someone come in, he would run to the side door from the garage and stick his big head through it as if to say, "Hey, what did you get me? Hurry, I want to come in and see! And oh, by the way, here's a kiss, too, while you're trying to open the door."

The years went by too fast and by the time Nick was fifteen, his hips gave out on him. It was on the same day that Mark's mother had a heart attack. (We did not want to tell her that Nick was down and not able to get up.) We took him to the vet and he had said to take the dog home and see if we could coax him up.

For three days we did everything we could. I stayed with him all three days with his head in my lap, telling him how much we loved him. On the third day of his suffering we took him to the vet again and he told us all we could do was put him to sleep. As you can imagine, it had been a hard couple of days with Mark's mother in the hospital, and now this. It was one of the hardest things to do. We both stayed with Nick until he was gone, his head still on my lap. (Oh, I miss that dog. But all good things must come to an end.)

When we left the vet, I felt as though Nick had loaded up in the car with us. But then I thought, I've really lost it.

When we got home, we were both upset and just sat around that night. Mark and I were in the kitchen and heard the sound of a dog's toenails coming around the porch into the garage. We both turned around to see if Nick's big head would come through the cat door; it didn't and we both began to cry. About a day and a half later, we came home from the hospital and went to the kitchen for a sandwich. Both of us heard Nick's dog tags jingle, even though they were on his collar and it was still out in Mark's truck. We looked at each other and asked, "Did you hear that?"

From then on things started to happen. I'd be in bed and hear the cat door slap even though the cat was on my bed at the time. We heard Nick's dog tags daily. One night we were sitting at the kitchen table having iced tea when we heard Nick whine. Both of us said, "Oh, he wants a cookie." My husband said, "Hold on, Nick, I'm coming." He went to the door to see him, but he wasn't there. We both said to each other, "I know you heard that!"

Not long after that, my husband saw a neighbor whose dog had puppies and we got the runt of the litter. His name is Captain. After he came home with us, we didn't hear too much more from Nick.

Captain now wears Nick's collar and he is just like Nick. It is amazing. He acts like him and even looks like him, so I think Nick is still around and helped us raise the puppy.

Bonnie's Return

by Angelina Proctor

About eight years ago when my husband (who is in the Navy) and I were living in Jacksonville, Florida, I called an ad in the paper for a free dalmatian. They told me to come on out and see the dog, whose name was Bonnie. When I arrived at the house, the man could not find her. After about ten minutes he realized she was under the house but would not come out when he called her.

I had been asking questions about her all the while and found out she'd had no veterinary care, no real diet for a dog (he mentioned she was given bologna the other day because they had no dog food), and that they really never wanted her in the first place. Finally, he went inside for a hot dog to try to lure her out. As soon as he left the yard, the dog shot out from under the house and leapt into my convertible, looking straight at me as if to say, "Hurry! Let's go before he comes back!"

Bonnie acted like she had always been a part of our family. Our shepherd, Charlie, took to her right away. At night both dogs slept on the floor at my side of the bed.

I took her to the vet right away and learned she had an advanced case of heartworms. We started treatment immediately. She seemed to be doing better until one day I mistakenly gave her the wrong pill. Bonnie became very ill and had to spend a week at the vet. She only did better when I went to visit her, so the vet decided that she was better off at home, and told me that her loneliness while there was overwhelming.

Before long, Bonnie could no longer walk. She passed away in her sleep. I was distraught and blamed myself for her death. Friends tried to comfort me, telling me she had found love at last and died in peace. My husband buried her in our backyard.

Not long afterward, we were lying in bed one night when we heard a dog's toenails on the wood floor in the hallway. And then our bedroom door, which was slightly ajar, was bumped open. I reached down and felt Charlie on the floor, sleeping soundly. My husband asked me if I had heard the toenails on the floor, too, and I said that I had and told him it was not Charlie.

I believe Bonnie was letting me know that everything was okay and I didn't need to blame myself. She loved me as I had loved her.

Suzy and the Phantom Puppy

by Crimson Willow

When I was twelve years old, we got a little mutt named Suzy. We found her on my grandma's farm, and she was the runt of the litter. She was a small dog—part beagle and part German shepherd.

Three years later, Suzy got pregnant. But alas, she had a miscarriage. She was very distraught and depressed after losing the puppy.

Two weeks after we buried the puppy in the backyard, Suzy

kept clamoring to go outside and play (she was mostly a house dog). She stayed outside for hours on end, and my siblings and I swore she was playing with her puppy that had passed on.

One night I sneaked outside to have a cigarette. I was sitting on the back porch steps when I heard a puppy whining. It sounded like it was coming from the far end of the backyard. I got up and walked over to see what the sound was. I could distinctly hear a puppy crying, and it sounded like it was cold and shivering. For the life of me, I could not find the source of the noise. I started to walk back to the porch, when I felt a tugging on my leg. I thought it was Suzy, since she was outside so much lately, but when I turned around and looked down, there was nothing there. Then I heard Suzy from inside the house, crying and scratching on the door to be let out. I let her out, and she proceeded to "play" in the corner where the sound of the puppy was coming from. This occurred for a few years before she finally went back to being her old self.

Suzy passed away when I was twenty-eight years old. When it occurred, she was still living with my parents in my childhood home. A year after it happened, I came for a visit and could have sworn I heard her toenails clicking in the kitchen. Not thinking, I said, "Come here, Suzy," and put my hand beside the couch for her to lick it, which had been our little ritual when I came home and sat in that particular couch. I had forgotten she had passed away, and I felt a lick on my hand. My mother was shocked and said, "Did you see that? Suzy is here." And I said, "I know, she's licking my hand." And that was when I realized that she was no longer of this realm.

This incident led us to talk about Suzy and all the good memories we had of her. Suzy had a habit of coming into the living room when everyone was watching television, farting, and then leaving the room with her tail between her legs. It made the whole family laugh; we covered our noses and yelled at her mockingly. As we laughed and talked about this memory, a stench came from under the table, and once again, we could hear her little nails clicking on the kitchen floor as she walked back to her box.

During this same visit home, I found my daughter playing in the backyard where we had buried the puppy. I noticed that it looked like she was running around in circles as if being chased by a dog. When she was done and came back inside, I asked her what she had been doing. She said, "Mommy! I was playing with Suzy and her puppy. You never told me that Suzy had a puppy."

Those were the last encounters I had with Suzy. I believe that she was saying good-bye to my daughter and me, and my parents never saw her ghost again after that visit.

Sullivan

by Erik Bratlien

My wife and our beloved golden retriever, Sullivan, were very close, almost as if they were of a kindred spirit. She bought Sullivan for me for Father's Day in 2003. But it quickly became evident who Sullivan wanted to be with most. He loved everyone in the family without complaint, but he had an otherworldly connection with my wife. They went everywhere together—on long walks and for long drives in the car.

My wife suffers from depression and Sullivan had been a godsend for her. When she was feeling bad, Sullivan was right there to comfort her. I know dogs try to comfort humans if they see them crying, but my wife wouldn't be crying. She was very closed up and quiet, and Sullivan could sense that she was feeling sad. He would not leave her side for any reason, not even to eat or drink. It was as if he was there to protect her and to watch over her.

When my wife suffered a severe valley of depression, the dog stayed by her side and nudged her with his nose. She gave him a little smile and he would lie back down.

Sullivan started to develop seizures. The vet ran tests to determine the cause and how to best deal with the seizures. I asked the vet if Sullivan had a thyroid problem, and he said the dog was too young to have a problem like that. He determined it was epilepsy, but I didn't think so. We had to give Sullivan medicine every day to control the seizures; he would have one every thirty days almost like clockwork. He began to have trouble keeping food down so we took him to a specialist and, without checking the dog out, he said, "I bet he has a thyroid problem." A blood test proved that he did. The specialist said the dog was also suffering from mega-esophagus, a condition in which all the nerves in the throat go dead and the dog can't keep anything down. Well, being a golden retriever he was too big to force-feed every few hours.

My wife tried to do the force feeding; she wanted to believe he was getting better and that I was wrong and that he didn't need to be put down. I could look into Sullivan's eyes and tell he wanted it to end. But even when he was hurting so badly, he was there trying to comfort my wife with her decision to put him down. She was finally able to see he was suffering and that he wanted it to end. We put him down on May 5, 2005.

When we returned home I walked into the bathroom to get my wife a tissue to blow her nose with. I found the cat's food dish, which we kept on the bathroom counter, laying on the floor. It had been on the counter and I had filled it up before we left to have Sullivan put down. The cats had never once knocked the dish off the counter, but Sullivan used to do it all the time. Later that evening while watching TV, my wife and I heard the noise of dog tags clinking, even though there wasn't a dog in the house and all of the windows were closed.

That night, after we went to bed and I turned off the lights, the bedroom door swung open and we heard and felt a dog wiggling under our bed like our golden retriever used to do. My wife gave me a smile and tears welled up in her eyes. I kissed her on her forehead and held her all night long. That was the first sign I noticed that our beloved Sullivan was still around. It was his way of letting us know he had come to visit.

On October 7, 2005, I noticed the dish on the floor again and I heard a dog bark at our back sliding-glass door. I thought it was our new dog, Max, but he was sound asleep in my wife's sewing room with her. I thought that was weird. Another night we were watching a movie and I heard a dog in the kitchen. I hollered, "Max, get in here!" My wife, who was sitting on the couch, said, "He is asleep right next to me." I quickly looked for all the cats, and all three of them were sitting on the couch by my wife. I looked at my stepson and he had heard it also.

To this day, every once in a while we hear the cat food dish in the bathroom hit the floor and the cat food spill all over. All the cats are accounted for right afterward to rule them out, and our new dog is sound asleep when it happens.

Sullivan is still around and even in death he is here to comfort; he is letting us know it will be okay.

The Sailor's Dog

by Gerina Dunwich

The spirit of a black Labrador retriever is said to haunt the South Bay Mariner's Cemetery in Port Milford, Ontario (Canada). According to local legend, the dog was the faithful companion of a sailor who died an accidental death aboard a schooner moored at Port Milford. The dog, which never abandoned its master's grave, pined away and now haunts the cemetery. Still mourning for its long-departed master, the ghostly Labrador can sometimes be heard howling in the dark of the night.

Forgiveness

by Robert Cruz

Chica was half-chow and half-beagle. I got her when I was fifteen.

I still remember the day she had to be put to sleep. I was up the street at a friend's house, when my mother stopped by with Chica in the car and asked me if I wanted to say good-bye to Chica. I told her no, I didn't care about her. I think now when I look back I just wanted to look tough in front of my friends.

Months went by after Chica was put to sleep. One night while going to sleep I heard a scratching noise at the door. But every time I looked to see what it was I saw nothing. When I finally went back to bed I heard the noise again, but this time I paid no attention to it.

I just tried to go to sleep. I heard the noise again and this time the sound was right by my bed. It sounded like a dog scratching on the wall. I was scared to open my eyes, but then I heard a dog breathing with excitement, the way dogs do when they're about to get a treat.

Finally I opened my eyes and there, I swear to God, was my dog Chica, licking me and wagging her tail so happily. I couldn't believe what was going on. But (it gets even stranger) there with Chica was a boy around twelve years old. He told me Chica wanted to say good-bye to me. He said not to worry, that he would take good care of her. The boy then said to Chica, "Come on, girl, we have to go," and Chica jumped off the bed and went with him.

I will never forget the look she gave to me with her tongue hanging down. And then, all of a sudden, they disappeared. I got up and even looked outside, but I couldn't find them. I was scared and happy at the same time. I went and woke up my mother and told her what had happened and she told me that Chica really cared for me.

I regret the day I didn't say good-bye to her, but I believe she came back to forgive me.

The Messenger

by Brenda Pelletier

Pat and I have been good friends for many years now. She had two pugs that have since passed on. I never met the first one, but I knew Willie. He was a cute loving little pug that grew to love me through the few years that I knew him. Willie used to love to sit on my lap when I visited. I brought him goodies; his favorite was cherry tomatoes.

At the age of sixteen, Willie became very sick with a brain tumor and passed on. It was such a sad day. Pat, who is unmarried and whose dogs were her life, held his urn for hours and rocked him and cried.

One day, about two weeks after Willie's death, I was doing dishes. I looked up and through the window by the sink I saw a little pug that looked just like Willie walk by with his tail wagging. He looked so happy and well. I thought a dog had gotten in the yard even though our backyard is fenced in. It took me by surprise. I ran outside and looked for this dog, but there was none!

I knew then it was Willie. I also knew he wanted me to tell his "mommy" that he was happy and well and for her not to cry anymore.

It took me a month to tell this to Pat, but when I did she couldn't understand why Willie didn't go to her. I don't understand it either, but I feel that he chose me to be his messenger.

I'll remember the day Willie appeared to me for the rest of my life. I was convinced there is life after death.

Eternal Love

by Tamara Buchfelder

I had an extremely tumultuous childhood that began to ease somewhat with the arrival of a very special Saint Bernard named Sandy. She belonged to one of my mother's friends, who was moving to Alaska. Because of Sandy's hip dysplasia, she feared the dog would not tolerate such a harsh climate, so she left Sandy with my family.

Sandy became my best friend; we were inseparable. She helped me through many of the hard paths of my childhood and was uncannily wise. She was also a fervent protector.

Due to her medical condition, she was put down when I was about fifteen years old. It was the saddest day of my life. Nobody had loved me as Sandy had.

Time moved on, and I became an adult. In my twenties, I went to see a psychic, and her first comment to me was that I was accompanied by a large dog, who stayed close to my side! Of course, I knew this to be Sandy, but I had not experienced any signs of her still being present in my life. This was to change a few years later.

As I entered my thirties, I was dating a man, who, at the time, seemed a good match for me. I was living alone in a two-story condo in a neighborhood that didn't have many dogs. I decided, after a few years, to give my boyfriend a key to my home so that we could share breakfast in the morning before heading to work.

The very first morning my boyfriend decided to use his key, I was sound asleep and not expecting him. Suddenly, I was awakened by the sound of a dog—a very large dog—barking frantically in my upstairs hallway! The barks were echoing in the high ceiling hall area; there was no mistake they were coming from *inside* my house! It took me a moment to register the fact that I did not have a dog.

As I very shakily arose from my bed, the barking ceased. I was now wide awake and wondering if I had hallucinated the entire episode. Meanwhile, downstairs at my back kitchen door, my boyfriend was frozen in suspended animation and terror, for at the very moment he had put the key to the lock, he heard the unmistakable barking of a very large, very ferocious dog inside my home.

I believe that Sandy was attempting to warn me of an intruder (and, as I eventually found out, a questionable character). After ruling out any other possibility and having two people hear the same thing, I can only conclude that my beloved friend really is still watching over me—even if I don't see signs of it every day. Eternal love apparently knows no bounds.

Wally

by Paul King

When I was a young teenager, my parents took in a miniature schnauzer named Wally when his original owner passed away. He was a great dog who got along well with everyone whether they were human or animal.

Each night after I went to bed, he jumped up beside me and lay against my legs for comfort and warmth. He lived with us for about two years or so when suddenly his kidneys failed and he had to be put to sleep. This upset me horribly and I cried for a couple of days.

A couple of nights after he passed away I was lying in my bed feeling about as low as one could imagine, when I felt something small jump into bed and immediately lean up against my legs. I looked down and there wasn't anything visible there, but I knew it was Wally coming back to tell me that he was okay and that everything was going to be all right. A great sense of peace came over me and I fell asleep in about five minutes.

I never felt Wally get into bed with me again. I believe he is now with his original owners, but I will never forget how he came back to let me know he was okay.

The Legend of Black Shuck

by *Gerina Dunwich*

Stories of a strange spectral dog known as Black Shuck abound in the folklore of the British Isles, and especially in the counties of Norfolk, Suffolk, and Cambridgeshire.

Those who claim to have witnessed this creature describe it as a large black dog, about the size of a calf, with glowing eyes of red, yellow, or green. Sometimes it appears with just a single gigantic eye in the middle of its forehead. It wears a collar of rattling chains around its neck and sometimes is headless. It has been seen running along or leaping across roads and often just vanishes into thin air.

Haunting cemeteries, back roads, misty marshlands, beaches, riverbanks, and the hills around villages, this mysterious phantom canine is believed by some to bring bad luck, madness, or death to any person unfortunate enough to lay eyes upon it or even hear its hellish howling. The curse it sends forth is said to manifest within twelve months. In parts of Devon, it is believed that misfortune befalls those who even speak of the hound. The people in Suffolk, however, believe that Black Shuck is only malevolent to persons who bother it. Some superstitious folks even think it to be the devil in disguise, as he is said to often appear in the form of a black dog.

In *The Encyclopedia of Ghosts and Spirits*, Rosemary Ellen Guiley writes, "On stormy nights, Black Shuck's bone-chilling howls can be heard rising above the wind. His feet make no sounds and leave no prints, but travelers feel his icy breath upon their necks." She also says it was the Black Shuck legends that inspired

Sir Arthur Conan Doyle to write his classic novel, *The Hound of the Baskervilles.*

Black Shuck is known by many other names, including Old Shuck (in Norfolk), Old Shock (in Suffolk), Old Snarleyow, Old Scarfe, Galleytrot, the Churchyard Beast, the Swooning Shadow, the Black Dog of Torrington, and Shug Monkey. It is interesting to note that the names "Shuck" and "Shock" are in fact derived from *succa,* an Old English word meaning demon.

The true origins of Black Shuck have since been lost in the mists of time. However, some believe the early Viking raiders inspired the legend of this supernatural beast with their tales of the black war hound of their god Odin. Others believe that Black Shuck was spawned by the ancient Welsh myth of Arawn, the ruler of the Underworld, whose "hounds of hell" roamed the night in search of human souls.

Black Shuck sightings have been reported for centuries, and continue in modern times, although not as frequently.

Spirit Guard Dog at Work

(anonymous)

My dad was a medium and I was raised to accept supernatural events. This has made me open to a lot of experiences, including one with the spirit of a guard dog.

There was an old bachelor who had a German shepherd named Miner. Wherever the man went, he took Miner with him. Miner guarded the truck when his master was in the store or away from the vehicle. If a woman passed by the truck, the dog was well behaved. But men were a different story, and he would not allow them to come near the truck. The only man who could get close to Miner was his owner.

In 1973 my husband and I moved into the apartment once occupied by Miner and the old bachelor. It was also the place where the dog had died and been buried. In the backyard was a rectangular concrete border that had a flat stone that said: MINER AT REST.

Only Miner didn't rest.

I was pregnant at the time and I believe Miner's spirit protected me when I was home. My husband could come in and out all day long and we never heard a thing, but at night it was a different story. If we left and came back after dark, I always had to go into the apartment first because Miner would not let my husband in until I went in and turned on the light. Only then could he come in. If my husband did try to go in first we both would hear serious growling, and we did not have a pet of any kind.

It was not an easy pregnancy for me and I tired easily. I often went to bed early. Miner did not let my husband in the bedroom if I were lying down after dark either. With the lights off, he sounded ready to attack. I would get up and turn on the bedroom light so that my husband could come in and get in bed and then I would turn off the light and go back to bed.

My husband and I are believers and didn't want to see what would happen if he ever crossed the line and entered the apartment or the bedroom at night first. I think it wouldn't have been pleasant. The funny part to me was I felt totally protected there, whereas my husband felt if he had ever raised his voice to me or showed any aggression to me he wouldn't have been safe.

What I never understood was why Miner's spirit stayed at that apartment instead of following his owner when the man moved away, because the man was still alive when we lived there, and Miner loved that man. I have a few pets that have crossed over and they have moved with me and I sometimes see their "shadows" and feel them around me.

Our Ghost Puppy

by Shannon M. Rea

In November of 2001, my Jack Russell terrier, Kodie, had a litter of five beautiful puppies. Unfortunately, one puppy did not make it. My family and I mourned the loss of this little male puppy and buried him the next morning.

Three days later, we took the rest of the litter to the vet to have their tails docked and dew claws removed. About five weeks later, the puppies had all the enthusiasm that puppies have and they were allowed to run around the living room on their own.

After a hard afternoon of playing and eating, it was time for a nice long nap. The puppies snuggled together in a pile to enjoy their companionship. Their mother, who was looking pretty worn out, and I were sitting on the couch enjoying a quiet moment. We sat there for about ten minutes when I heard the distinct sound of a distressed puppy coming from the bathroom. Kodie's ears perked up, her body tensed, and she stared in the direction of the unmistakable sound of a panicked puppy.

It was not unusual for one of the puppies to go into a room, have the door swing shut, and after realizing they were separated from the rest of their brothers and sisters, start to whine and yelp until one of us "saved" them.

As I was getting up to rescue the little adventurer from the closed bathroom, I glanced at the pile of sleeping puppies and counted four. I froze in place for a moment at the realization that there was not a puppy stuck in the bathroom. I looked at Kodie and she was still motionless and tense. Her ears were alert, and she was staring at the door. I counted the puppies again just to make sure I didn't miss any. All four of them were fast asleep in a pile across the room.

That was the start of some very strange puppy encounters at my home.

About three weeks later, after all of my little sweetie pies had found wonderful homes, I let Kodie out in the yard so that I could vacuum (she despises the vacuum and will bark, chase, and bite at it until I'm done). As I was focused on vacuuming, I caught a glimpse of a Jack Russell puppy with an undocked tail sniffing the floor by the bathroom door (the same bathroom that Kodie and I heard the puppy in). The only puppy in the litter that didn't have its tail docked was the little male that didn't make it.

My family couldn't help but believe that the puppy we lost was somehow still with us! We saw and heard the ghost puppy in the living room from time to time, until we moved in August of 2005.

Sampson and Teddy

by Russell Roberts

I live in the Utica area of central New York in a house built circa 1805. My grandparents, who used to live in the house, had two dogs that they adopted in the 1970s. Sampson (my favorite of the two dogs) was a white-and-brown-spotted English spaniel with a bobbed tail. The other dog, Teddy, was a black-and-tan-colored terrier mix. The two dogs got along well, despite being from separate homes. They are buried on a hill just off the back lawn within view of the house.

My story about these dogs starts two years ago when my girlfriend Elizabeth was visiting my home and asked who the two dogs looking in the window were. I looked and didn't see anything. But I knew from experience that she was able to see things in the ghostly realm reflected in television screens or windows.

I might add that from my own experiences with ghosts I have taken up the hobby of ghost hunting as a way to prove and document the existence of ghosts, especially through photography. One day I saw a dog's head in a picture I took inside the house. Later I saw two dogs in exterior pictures I took and they strongly resembled the two dogs that had belonged to my grandfather.

Last winter I heard a dog bark twice in the hallway while I was working on the computer. It sounded just like Sampson's bark. (As I remember, he usually would bark twice and had a deeper bark than the other dog.) Upon investigation I found no dogs in the area, either inside or outside. So I figured Sampson was just letting me know of his presence or wanted me to do something for him, which I could not do being unable to see him.

It's nice to know that both dogs loved living here enough to stay around even after their physical lives ended.

Man's Best Friend, Even in the Afterlife

by Doris "Dusty" Smith

At one time, the most popular resident of the Daytona Beach downtown business area was not human. I will now tell you about the most popular goodwill ambassador Daytona Beach has ever had. I am speaking of a dog that came to be called Brownie.

It seems that this weary yet wise traveler somehow made his way to Daytona Beach. Like many before him, and many more after him, Brownie explored the sidewalks and storefronts of Beach Street for several days before staking a claim. Brownie's first and soon to become best friend was Ed Budgen, Sr. Ed was the owner of the Daytona Cab Company, located on the corner of Orange Avenue and Beach Street. When Brownie met Ed, Ed offered Brownie part of his lunch. Now being the smart and resourceful dog he was, Brownie gladly accepted the free meal.

Brownie quickly learned how to capitalize on this gracious human trait. Many of the downtown workers and restaurant owners fed Brownie scraps on a regular basis. Brownie took up residency at the Daytona Cab Company with his new friend Ed, who even made him a doghouse from a cardboard box. Eventually Brownie's home became a bit more upscale; it was quite elaborate, complete with Brownie's name on it. A collection box was added, and many people donated to the "Brownie care fund." This fund provided food, veterinary care, and money for Brownie's annual license. C. P. Miller made sure that every year Brownie got tag #1, since Brownie was the goodwill ambassador for Daytona Beach.

One local resident remembers that Brownie took up residence in 1940. At this time downtown shopping was popular. He quickly became known as "the town dog." It was customary on a shopping spree to see and greet Brownie. His reply would always be a wag of his tail. One of the benefits to being the "town dog" was an occasional free pint of ice cream, which Brownie cherished.

Brownie became a trusted companion to many of the local cab drivers. He took it upon himself to accompany the police patrolmen on their nightly rounds. Brownie assisted the officers by sniffing at shadows in dark alleys and standing at the side of officers while the local businesses' doors were checked.

Brownie's fame grew, but his ego didn't, even after being written up in national magazines and newspapers as "Daytona Beach's dog." Many visiting tourists would seek out Brownie as they walked and shopped along Beach Street; they wanted to have their picture taken with the country's most popular dog. Ed's wife Doris remembers Brownie getting Christmas cards and presents from all over the country. Doris would respond on Brownie's behalf and include a photo of the now famous dog.

Brownie passed of old age in October of 1954. Many of the fine folks from across the country felt the loss and sent letters and cards of condolence. Brownie's bank account had enough money in it to construct a plywood casket and purchase a headstone. City officials provided a resting place in Riverfront Park, which is directly across from the place where Brownie had spent the best years of his life.

There were seventy-five people in attendance, with four pallbearers, at Brownie's funeral. As Mayor Jack Tamm stated in Brownie's eulogy, "Brownie was, indeed, a good dog," as many shed a tear.

Now that I have told you about Brownie's life in this world, let me tell you how I met Brownie in the next world. On one of our little outings, I decided it might be worthwhile to go and visit Brownie's resting place. We arrived at Riverfront Park at about 11 p.m. I took off in one direction; two fellow researchers went in the opposite direction. Now normally we stick together, but we had no idea exactly where Brownie was buried. Riverfront Park is quite large with many fishponds, small footpaths and bridges, and beautiful gardens. I walked to the south; the others went north. My radar must have been in tune that night because I walked straight to Brownie's place of rest.

When I turned around to see where the other researchers had gone, they were completely out of sight. I decided to have a little chat with Brownie and take a few pictures. I of course introduced myself and explained to him that I had read about how famous and humble he had been. I noticed the shrub to the north of his headstone was supposed to be in the shape of a dog, but was a bit lacking. (Boxwoods can be hard to train sometimes.) Anyhow, I noticed how wonderfully done Brownie's headstone was. And the Mayor's quote inscribed at the bottom, A GOOD DOG.

As I stood there thinking about this goodwill ambassador and what a wonderful impact he had on this town and the folks who were lucky enough to encounter him, I suddenly felt sad. I wondered how many people still remembered this fine animal? Obviously the grass was mowed on a regular basis, but how many even knew of this location? Did someone still come and talk to Brownie? Did anyone ever bring him flowers or maybe lay a dog biscuit down for him? Did Brownie still recall what it felt like to be petted? Or what ice cream tasted like?

My belief is that we take these feelings and thoughts onto the other side with us. How sad would it be if no one remembered us? I realize that in a hundred years there would be no one around to remember whom and how we really were. But, couldn't someone make the afterlife a little special for this obviously special dog? Yep, you're right, it would be me! I decided at that moment to take Brownie on as my very own spirit pet. I would visit him as often as I could. Talk to him, offer him biscuits, or as they are known in my house, "cookies." I've come to a point in my relationship with my own dog that I have to spell out the "c" word or she won't leave me alone until she gets one.

I noticed a park bench near Brownie's place of rest. It seemed to be so inviting. Sitting on a park bench, dog at your side, listening to the wind and watching the traffic go by. I told Brownie that if he cared to join me, I would be more than happy to sit with him for a while. After several minutes, I felt warmth at my left leg. Could it have been Brownie? Or was it just a warm breeze coming in off the intercoastal waterway? Just then I noticed the other researchers headed my way. The warmth was gone. I spoke to Brownie again, "Thank you for taking time to sit with me. I needed to feel a loyal friend tonight. I do hope you will reveal yourself in a picture. You *are* a good dog," I said. I snapped a picture of where I had been sitting with what I felt was my new friend, Brownie, the spirit dog. I looked at the LCD screen on the digital camera and noticed a bright orb in front of the palm tree. Nah, it couldn't be. . . . I couldn't get that lucky. We decided to say our "good nights" to Brownie and walk back through the park to the car.

When we returned to home base and viewed the digital photos I was delighted. Not only had we gotten some decent orb activity, Brownie had made his presence known. The picture I had taken of the park bench featured a beautiful orb in front of the palm tree. I looked at it for less than two seconds before realizing it had a face in it. Not an ordinary face though, Brownie's face! You can call me nuts at any time, but I know the face in the orb is Brownie.

It seems to me that this famous goodwill ambassador is still doing his job. Sitting next to visitors or weary travelers in a cool shady corner of the park. Keeping an eye on the passing traffic. Walking alongside pets that still reside in this world. Maybe even romping through the park to visit with otherworldly residents of the park. Whatever the case, Brownie is still doing his job, and he will always be, a good dog.

Benny

by Jaclyn Reay

My dog, Benny, was my best friend. He was half Jack Russell and half Chihuahua, and was given to me when I was seven years old. We did everything together.

When I got older and went to high school, Benny found it hard to keep calm when I'd not return home at my normal hour. If I went out with friends or to an after school project, he got so stressed that sometimes he would try to escape to find me.

I moved to Sydney, Australia, soon after turning eighteen, and whenever I came home to see my parents (who lived on a farm outside of town), Benny was excited to see me. I spent every waking moment I could with him. We were inseparable until I had to leave and return to the city.

One day in July of 2005, Benny went missing. He was so old now that he got tired after a five-minute stroll. And he was also going blind and deaf, so he couldn't have wandered off too far. But despite the best efforts of my family, we couldn't find him, or his remains either.

I was grief-stricken and cried for days over losing my best friend. Fearing that I had let him down, I went and saw a medium . . . by accident. I thought this woman gave career guidance but she gave more "life guidance" instead. She told me that Benny is fine and that he sits outside where my mother often sits. (My mother is a smoker and would sit on the back veranda where Benny had his sleeping blanket.) She told me to not worry and that he was there and knew that I loved him very much. He didn't want me to see him die, so he wandered off and did it quietly.

When I visited my parents again, I was lying in bed and could hear Benny walking around on the veranda right outside my window. I feel his presence every time I go home and I'm glad he is still with me, even though not physically. I miss Benny but I know he's sitting there keeping my mother company.

The Wild Hunt

by Gerina Dunwich

The Wild Hunt, according to the folklore of the British Isles, is a phantom procession of mounted huntsmen and baying black hellhounds, which, at times, appear headless. Sometimes led by Herne the Hunter, the goddess Hecate, or even the devil himself, these dreadful specters roam about the countryside, cloaked in the darkness of night, in search of human souls.

It is said that bad luck befalls all persons who lay their eyes upon this procession, unless they immediately fall to the ground and recite the Lord's Prayer to save their souls. But those who are foolish enough to speak to any of the huntsmen can be sure to expect a visit from Death. Some folks also believe that the earthbound souls of the unbaptized dead—particularly infants—are chased to hell by the dogs of the Wild Hunt.

In Cornwall, the huntsmen's hounds are known as the Devil's Dandy Dogs, and persons who claim to have seen them say the pack runs along the ground or sometimes just above it. One account from the twelfth century estimated the number of huntsmen to total between twenty and thirty.

All Hallows' Eve and nights wrought by stormy weather and howling winds are believed to be the times when the Wild Hunt commences. And on such nights, all who dare to venture out are warned to do so only with the utmost caution, lest the phantom hounds snatch up their souls and carry them off to hell.

Ghost Dogs and Tears of Blood

by R. Mallard

Being born and raised in Savannah, Georgia, I have always had a great fascination for this area's local urban legends and ghost stories.

On the east side of the city lies the old Bonaventure Cemetery, which dates back to the eighteenth century when it was a family cemetery on a plantation. Before being purchased by the city of Savannah in the year 1907, it was called the Evergreen Cemetery. Many Civil War soldiers and even some famous people (like

Johnny Mercer and Conrad Aiken) are buried there. And in 1994, a murder mystery called *Midnight in the Garden of Good and Evil* partly took place at this historic burial ground.

The cemetery is believed to be haunted by a pack of ghost dogs that roam the grounds after the sun goes down. Some of the braver souls who have walked through the cemetery after dark have reported being chased by invisible phantom hounds. The dogs have never been seen by anyone, but they can be heard barking and panting.

Back when I was a youngster in college, I heard another supernatural story about Bonaventure (which, incidentally, means "good fortune" in French). I was told that there's a statue there that overlooks the grave of a young child and weeps tears of blood. The legend of this statue is so well known that many people come to the cemetery just to place flowers, money, or little trinkets of some kind in the palms of the statue's hands.

The Spaniel Specter

by James Griffiths

Usually when a psychic is called in to "clean" a place it is because the people who live there don't like the spirit and it's causing problems. I was asked about three weeks ago to help someone with a problem in their home. They were worried about their daughter; she had been hearing things, feeling cold spots in the apartment, and seeing shadows and other things.

When I arrived, I knocked on the door and was welcomed in by the gentleman of the house; his wife was in the kitchen. As I walked toward the kitchen I felt something touch my forearm. I carried on in and asked, "Do you want me to tell you if there is a spirit here or if you're going round the twist?" (I know, very "professional." But some people feel they are going mad, so if a medium confirms there is spirit there, they are happy.) I sat in the kitchen and looked to the hallway. I could see shadows moving about but just watched. I was also drawn to the door at the bottom of the hall, where I felt knocking and banging had been heard.

I asked them if I could go to that room at the bottom of the hall and they said, "Yes. My daughter's room is down there, too." I walked down to this room but could not feel anything, so I turned around to walk into their daughter's room. On this particular night I had a camera with me, and as I walked into her room, something jumped up at me and knocked the camera out of my hand. It flew across the room and landed on the floor. I thought to myself, Great I have broken that camera now. I looked around the room to see or feel if there was anything in there. Right at the bottom of the bed was a dog, or rather the back of a dog. As I looked at its coat, which was shining, everything seemed to connect with the goings on of this house.

I walked back into the kitchen and by now the daughter had arrived home. She was young, only about sixteen or seventeen. I said, "Hi, are you okay?" I could see she had fear in her eyes. I don't know if it was fear of the ghost or me.

I asked if they ever had a dog that was a King Charles spaniel with cream and red or brown fur, and they said yes. I then asked if they had heard scratching on the doors and had seen shadows in the bedroom, and again their reply was yes. "Well, let me tell you, it's your dog that is here," I said. "Also there are a couple of your family members here at the moment to speak to you."

149

After I gave the messages, I walked back into the room and cleansed it and lifted the energies and advised the family what to do with the room after I left. I also told them about the dog meeting me at the door and jumping up at me and knocking my camera out of my hands. The owners said that these were the habits of this particular dog. They said they could not go anywhere without her following or jumping on them.

About five days later I received an e-mail from the lady, who said, "Thank you for putting our minds at rest. But one question: How do you keep a spirit dog off your bed when you don't want dog hairs on your sheets?"

I said, "That's one for a vet to answer."

4

OTHER GHOSTLY ANIMALS

The Phantom Carriage of Lookout Mountain Road

by Gerina Dunwich

Up in the Hollywood hills, above the hustle and bustle of the city and not far from the allegedly haunted ruins of Harry Houdini's old burned-out mansion, lies the intersection of Laurel Canyon Boulevard and Lookout Mountain Road. It is an area of frequent ghost sightings. In the summer of 2000, I was hired to do tarot readings for a birthday party at a house on Lookout Mountain Road. It turned out to be quite a festive event, lasting for about six hours and attended by actress Fairuza Balk and many other people who worked in the entertainment industry. Around midnight, it began to break up.

After collecting my payment, I packed up my Rider-Waite deck, got into my car, and began heading home. Within minutes I reached the bottom of Lookout Mountain and then turned left onto Laurel Canyon Boulevard. It was at that moment that I spotted an old-fashioned carriage pulled by two white horses racing madly down Lookout Mountain Road toward the intersection. Oddly, there was no galloping sound.

The silent apparition lasted for only a second or two before vanishing into thin air. At the time I thought I had simply imagined it due to the fact that I was extremely tired and my eyes were strained from hours of card readings. However, I later discovered that other people had also witnessed the same thing at the very same location.

Upon further research, I also learned that this apparition was said to be responsible for a number of traffic accidents at the intersection of Laurel Canyon and Lookout Mountain Road. Apparently some drivers, upon seeing the phantom carriage suddenly appear, slam on their brakes or swerve to avoid hitting it, resulting in a collision with other vehicles.

The Silver Wolf

by *Karen Simpson*

My daughter, Krista Simpson, has been seeing spirits since she was a young child. The following story, which she told to me, is an account of the very first and only time she ever saw an animal spirit.

One evening during an electrical storm, Krista was lying on the couch, looking out the living room window and enjoying the natural beauty of the lightning show. Suddenly, out of the corner of her eye she began to see a glow, almost as if someone had turned on a light in the room. It struck her as odd. She slowly turned her head to get a better view of the source without looking directly at whatever it was. (Krista had always avoided looking directly at the spirits as they scare her horribly, but something about this one made her want to look at it more fully.) What she saw amazed her. It was a beautiful silvery metallic glow that was very strong and very bright.

This intrigued her so she turned her head further and saw a beautiful, silvery wolf. Its coloring was like that of a Siberian husky, and she knew it was definitely a spirit because there was transparency to it.

It startled her to see a wild animal such as this in our home, but this wolf seemed to be more domesticated. He looked strong and proud and very beautiful. His eyes were brilliant. The glow he radiated was much stronger than that of any other spirits she had witnessed before.

As Krista lay on the couch she began to sense something about the animal. He seemed to be protecting something. She noticed the direction of the animal's concentrated stare. It seemed to be looking just over her shoulder at the wall behind her. She felt that she was safe in his presence and could relax. She also sensed that what he was protecting had something to do with people but she did not know whether it was someone from the past or us.

As a little more time passed, Krista began to sense more about this beautiful creature. She sensed the name of the animal was Nabdon and that it meant her no harm. This relaxed her as she continued to try to watch it from the corner of her eye. Nabdon stood without moving for a short period of time. He did not move from his original spot nor did he make any type of noises. Suddenly the glow began to dim and the wolf was gone just as quickly as he had appeared.

I have done research on his name and tried to discover where this animal might have come from and whom he was protecting, but could find nothing.

Our home is old and has stood on the same spot for nearly a hundred years. This general area is very rich in Indian and Colonial history, and most of the ghosts encountered by Krista have been those of Colonial-era men, women, and children. She has also witnessed Civil War soldiers as well as more modern individuals, but never before had she ever seen the spirit of an animal such as the silver wolf.

My Cougar Spirit Guide
by Eileen Smith

The following story concerns an animal spirit guide, which is also called a totem or power animal. It happened when I was under apprenticeship to a shaman who taught both Peruvian and Native American shamanism. It was a traditional apprenticeship that lasted years and required much emotional and spiritual work on the part of the apprentice.

I was going through what is called a Medicine Wheel, which takes several years to complete. During one portion, or "direction" of it, I was in a forest with the shaman. One night after going to bed, I had a very vivid dream of a cougar up high on a large overhanging tree branch staring down at me. She slinked down and jumped to the ground, her eyes on me all the time. She came up to me and bit my hand. I grabbed my hand in pain and saw three puncture marks oozing blood.

When I awoke, I immediately looked to my hand, because it was still in pain. I expected to see puncture wounds because the dream was so vivid. But there was not a mark on it. During break-fast I told my shaman teacher what had happened and, in excite-ment, the shaman told me that I had been "marked," that it was an initiation by my power animal.

For days that hand hurt. It was as if the puncture wounds in my dreams were throbbing but just could not be seen. Not long after, I became a healer. Many of those who can see spirits see a large wild cat walking by my side or close by. In my own visions, meditations, and abilities, I have formed a close bond with this powerful cougar spirit.

In a related story, I purchased a statue in honor of my cougar spirit, and people who saw it swore that its glass eyes moved and watched them. I had seen it, but thought it may be my imagina-tion, until others saw it, too. A psychic once came over and saw the statue and said a large cat lived within it.

One night, years later, the glass eyes looked so real I took my camera to take a picture of them. A voice in my head said, "Don't take a picture," yet I did anyway. The next morning, the statue fell and smashed. I had had it for years and was very upset. I glued it together, but the spirit never dwelled in it again.

I believe my cougar spirit may have entered into the statue when I purchased it. My cougar is still with me, but does not use the statue anymore, although I wish it would. It was rather special to have it show itself like that to others and me.

Sir Cedric the Guinea Pig

by Toby Longbrake

Although I had one pot-bellied pig, three geese, two dogs, and four cats, I felt I had a giant void in my life when I lost my first pot-bellied pig to liver failure. I had been on permanent disability for about six months when my daughter came over to my house with a baby guinea pig. It took about one minute for me to fall in love with the little guy. My husband told me I had enough animals, but finally gave in to letting me keep the guinea pig, which I named Sir Cedric.

He slept in a cage at night, and each morning I took him out and put him in a playpen with his little house and plastic tubes. Whenever I walked into the room, he whistled. I would say to him, "Let me give you a kiss," and he would turn his head so I could kiss his cheek. He would kiss me too.

I had Sir Cedric for about a year and a half before he became ill. I knew that once guinea pigs get sick they usually die. I sat up with him all night and then took him to the vet in the morning. He gave Cedric some medicine and instructed me to give him apple juice. I sat up with him the next night and, lo and behold, he survived!

About three months later he became ill again. But this time he didn't make it. I was devastated. I know the tears I had shed were for a rodent, but like the vet once said; you can't help what your heart loves.

A few days later I was sitting in the living room when I saw Sir Cedric run across the room. I thought maybe I had lost my mind, so I didn't say anything about it to anyone. A few days after that, my grandson said he saw a rat with no tail that looked just like Sir Cedric. Since then my husband has seen him, too.

The Sabino Canyon Mountain Lion

by Gerina Dunwich

A phantom mountain lion or "wildcat" is said to haunt Sabino Canyon in the Coronado National Forest of Tucson, Arizona. It reportedly appears after sundown and stalks those who stray from the paved main road. Its presence has been described as "heavy" and "negative," and persons who have witnessed this apparition while hiking or jogging through the area have said it appeared to be angry. Little else is known about this animal anomaly.

A Horse Spirit Encounter

by Eyramon (as told to Tony Mierzwicki)

In Australia's old Colonial Days, nearly two hundred years ago, the white settlers introduced horses, some of which were released into the wild. These horses, known as "brumbies," became an integral part of Australian mythology and were widely employed by stockmen and troopers of the Australian light horse regiments. Brumbies were praised by numerous Australian writers for their stamina, intelligence, agility, and endurance. They were glorified in the closing ceremony of the 2000 Olympic games held in Sydney.

Three months after the Olympics, the New South Wales government sanctioned the culling of brumbies in the Guy Fawkes River National Park in the northern tablelands of NSW. The culling took place using automatic weapons from helicopters. Following worldwide condemnation of the culling, some of the surviving brumbies were rounded up.

One property in the vicinity of the National Park became the home for a "mob" (herd) of brumbies. The mob consisted of a bay lead stallion, other stallions, and a large group of mares, foals, and yearlings. The property owner tried in vain to control the lead stallion. After a year, the exasperated property owner gave up and had the lead stallion shot.

Two and a half months after the shooting, I was taken to the vicinity of the lead stallion's resting place in order to lay his spirit to rest. I was drawn unerringly to the scene of the killing, near the head of the valley. All that remained after exposure to the elements were the lead stallion's bones, as well as some mane and tail hair. I had felt his presence from the moment I started up the valley.

The presence grew stronger the closer I approached, culminating in an overwhelming feeling when I at last reached his remains. I reached down to pick up his skull. One of the teeth in the lower right mandible (jawbone) was loose in its socket. As I pulled it free, I felt an overpowering surge of energy enter me. I became possessed of the lead stallion's essence to the exclusion of my own personality. I then picked up some of his tail hair.

Holding the tooth and tail hairs, I attempted to release the lead stallion's spirit into the Summerland (afterlife), but he would not go. I was one with him and felt a part of me fly with him like Pegasus high over the earth that had borne us both. The remaining part of me remained grounded by his bones. I somehow finished the ritual and felt his gratitude. But, I was still possessed by his overwhelming presence.

I made my way back from the valley and approached the homestead, around which were small paddocks containing about thirty brumbies. As I approached they came up to me, sensing their leader's presence. A couple nuzzled my hand, which held the tooth and tail hair. They followed me along the fence. These horses were wild and had not been handled.

The owner came out of the homestead and hugged me, as if to convey his guilt for having had the lead stallion shot. The woman who had actually shot him scuttled rat-like across my path, and appeared to be an empty shell.

For me, this event marked the culmination of my spiritual path in this lifetime. The spirit of the lead stallion had merged with mine. My own horses and dogs acknowledge this, while wild creatures have no fear of me. I feel I have been transformed and am aware of the immortality of my essence. My experience was one of nirvana leading to a detached contentment I had never known before.

The Legend of England's Last Bear

by Gerina Dunwich

Legend has it that the last bear in England was killed in the forest near Verdley Castle, just south of Fernhurst, England. The animal's ghost is said to haunt the area; however, some folks claim that the apparition appears only once a year at Christmas.

Accompanied by an Australian film crew, a half-dozen psychic mediums (among them a psychic artist and a psychometric medium), and two historians met at the ruins of Verdley Castle in 2004 to film a documentary on animal ghosts. It was one of ten one-hour programs in a series about cryptozoology (the investigation of creatures whose existence is unproved), and its main purpose was to establish whether a ghostly bear presence existed in the Verdley Woods.

In order to prevent them from being subconsciously influenced, the psychics were not told anything beforehand about the legend of the ghost bear. The reason why the filmmakers were there was also not disclosed to them.

The filming began early in the evening and continued into the wee hours of the night. While on camera, the psychics walked around the site, each picking up different vibrations from the stones that remained of the ruined castle and from the area surrounding it. They talked about their psychic impressions and collectively covered a wide range of possible uses of the ruins that spanned several centuries.

One of the psychics sensed that the ruins were at one time used as a protective fortress, while another strongly felt they were connected to ancient religious practices. One received impressions that the place had once been a hunting lodge. And still another seemed sure it had something to do with the breeding of horses. However, none of the six psychics picked up anything having to do with the killing of a bear or of the animal's ghost.

My Dead Rabbit Haunted Me

by Rachel Schuetz

When I was nine years old, I received a rabbit as a pet from my parents, which I named Bunbun. I loved Bunbun with all my heart.

At night while I was asleep he crawled under my covers and sat in my arms until I awoke. If I were still asleep and late for school, he tugged on my shirt and clawed at it until I responded. Sometimes he lay next to my legs and watched TV with me. This continued for years.

At age seven, Bunbun died a long and painful death. We assumed he had a heart attack and liquid had filled his lungs. It took him all day to die, and at the end he cried for me. The night he died, I still felt as though he was hopping all over my bed, but I chalked that up to the grief.

Months passed and I soon got new rabbits. One night I was sleeping and awoke to a rabbit hopping around my head. Thinking it was one of my new rabbits, I thought nothing of it and turned on the light. I looked around my bed and saw nothing. I looked under it and both of my new rabbits had been lying under it the entire time. That was the first occurrence of Bunbun coming back. A few days later my mother was trying to take a nap and felt like someone was hopping all over her. She looked around and there was nothing to be seen.

Soon we had to split my two rabbits up until we could get them fixed, so one was in my mom's room and the other was in mine.

During that time the occurrences slowed down, but I would still occasionally feel something hopping on me.

Last Thanksgiving my grandfather died, and my family had to leave while I stayed at the house to take care of the rabbits. I was lying in bed one night, trying to sleep, when I felt hopping on my legs. I looked down and my bed was barren. The hopping continued until I felt the mass lie down next to my legs and shift its weight onto my legs just as Bunbun had always done. This continued until my family came back from the funeral.

Since then, I have never felt Bunbun again.

Pet Shop Ghosts

by Ed Murakami

After my retirement in the spring of 1995, my wife and I decided it would be fun to open a bookstore. Being avid readers, we had accumulated quite a number of books over the decades and felt that a shop would be the ideal way to downsize our gargantuan collection and make some room in our house. Being in business for ourselves was also something she and I had dreamed about for a very long time.

We scouted around for a while to find the right place, but soon discovered that most of the prices were way above what we could afford or the neighborhoods were unsafe or the buildings needed too much work. We were beginning to feel discouraged when luck smiled on us and we found a decent place not far from our home, priced just right! We signed the lease and set up business in what used to be a neighborhood pet shop. It was a dream come true for both of us, but it didn't take long before my wife and I started having odd experiences that defied all rational explanation.

The first of many such experiences occurred while I was in the shop doing inventory. I felt the sensation of something brushing against my ankle. I instinctively looked down but saw nothing. Another time I could have sworn that I heard the faint fluttering of wings. I made no mention of it until a few days later when my wife reported experiencing the same sort of things. She told me she sometimes felt like eyes were watching her, even when she and I were the only ones in the shop. She added that she also felt it when she was completely alone.

I tried to assure her that it was just her imagination getting the best of her. After all, we were both rational mature adults who were taught there was a logical explanation for everything. And neither of us was silly enough to believe in such things as ghosts . . . that is until the night we saw one with our very own eyes.

It was the day after Halloween and we were closing up shop for the evening. I had just switched off the lights and was heading out the door with my wife when something made me turn around and take a look. Lo and behold, there was something resembling a small animal sitting there on the counter near the cash register, and it was looking straight at me! It was a misty form, about the size of a large kitten or a small puppy, and its eyes seemed to glow in the dim light from the street that filtered through the front window of the shop. I thought my eyes must have been playing tricks on me. I uttered a "What the hell?" just as my wife turned and saw it, too. She gasped loudly and then I switched the lights back on. But whatever had been sitting there watching us just a moment before seemed to vanish in the light.

Since then my wife and I have opened our minds to matters

concerning ghosts and the afterlife. We have no fear of the entities that coexist with us in the shop because we realize they aren't there to harm us. In fact, we've come to affectionately think of them as our little invisible pets.

The Spectral Ape of Athelhampton House

by Gerina Dunwich

Located near Dorchester (in Dorset, England), the Tudor manor house known as Athelhampton House was built by Sir William Martyn in the year 1485. It is reputedly haunted by several ghosts, including one of a cooper that can be heard tapping away at barrels in the wine cellar, and a Grey Lady that has been observed wandering through the bedrooms in the east wing of the house. Witnesses have reported seeing her apparition appear and then vanish through the walls.

But the most famous (and perhaps oddest) specter that inhabits this house is that of a pet ape, which belonged to Nicholas Martyn in the sixteenth century. (Interestingly, the Martyns' family crest depicted an ape sitting on the stump of a tree, and the family motto was: "He who looks at Martyn's ape, Martyn's ape will look at him.")

The story goes that when Nicholas (the last of the Martyn line) passed away in 1595, the ape wandered about the house in search of its new master until it died. According to another story, the ape somehow ended up entombed behind a wall during construction work and either suffocated or starved to death. Unexplained scratching sounds have been heard coming from a secret staircase behind the paneling in the great chamber, and many have attributed this to the phantom ape. Some also believe the animal continues to roam the house in search of its long dead master.

On a final note, Athelhampton House, which was used for filming the Michael Caine film *Sleuth*, was also featured on *Most Haunted*, a popular British television show that conducts investigations in haunted houses and other locations where paranormal activity has been reported. While filming at the house, a number of mysterious orbs were captured on video.

The Gerbil That Came to Dinner

by Denise Healey

Back in the late sixties when my younger sister and I were still in grammar school, we had two pet gerbils named Bonnie and Clyde and a big striped tabby cat we called Bangles. One day my sister forgot to latch the door on the gerbils' cage and both of them got out and were scurrying through the house. With our father's help we managed to round up Clyde. Unfortunately, Bangles got to Bonnie before we did. After being pawed and tossed around in the air a few times, the poor little thing died of fright. With tears in our eyes, we buried her in the backyard, using an empty kitchen matchstick box as a coffin.

A few months down the road, our family had just sat down for supper when all of a sudden my mother let out a blood-curdling shriek and jumped onto the seat of her chair as fast as she could. At that instant a small furry thing about the same size and color as our dearly departed gerbil darted across the dining room floor and into the kitchen where it vanished from sight. Oddly, Bangles the cat did not chase after the rodent, but I did notice the fur on her back start to bristle as she watched it go by. My father scolded my sister for again leaving the cage door open, but she began to cry and insisted that she hadn't. When we went into the bedroom to check on the cage, we found the door securely latched and Clyde inside on his exercise wheel.

I remember saying that I thought Bonnie's ghost had returned from the dead and then my father reprimanding me for scaring "the daylights" out of my little sister. He insisted that what we had seen was just an ordinary mouse (although it sure looked a lot like Bonnie) and then went out and bought a bunch of mousetraps, which he baited with cheese and placed all around the house. But that was the last we saw of the little creature. About six months later, after no mouse had been caught, my mother tossed out all the traps and concluded that the cat must have scared the mouse away.

I never again brought up my gerbil ghost theory, but many times since then I've wondered to myself if maybe that elusive mouse, or whatever it was that scurried across the dining room floor that day, could actually have been the ghost of our little furry friend paying us all a very brief, but memorable, visit. As crazy as it might sound, I have a funny feeling that the only one who really knew for sure was Bangles.

The White Rabbit

by Mary Leroux

When I was a young girl my parents used to take me several times a year to visit my grandfather who lived in rural upstate New York. It was a good three-and-a half-hour drive from our home in Burlington, Vermont. I never minded the long trip, however, because on the way up we always stopped at the Johnsons' farm to buy honey or maple syrup and I would get to play with Elmer—their beautiful pet Angora rabbit with silky white hair.

I remember going to the farm one crisp autumn day. No sooner had my father put the car into park, than I was out the door and running straight to the rabbit hutch in the barn behind the Johnsons' house as I had done at least a dozen times before. When Elmer saw me approaching he stood up on his hind legs as if to greet me. I was anxious to pet him, as I loved how his soft fur felt against the palm of my hand. But as I started to open the door on the hutch, I heard my mother calling me. I told Elmer I'd be right back and then hurried to the front of the house. My parents and Mrs. Johnson were talking on the front porch and they all had a solemn look on their faces.

"What's the matter?" I asked, sensing that something was wasn't quite right.

"Honey," my mother said softly as she comfortingly put her arm around me, "Mrs. Johnson just gave us some sad news. It seems Elmer got very sick a couple months ago and now he's in heaven with God. I'm sorry, sweetie."

Confusion rippled through me. "No! That's not true!" I argued. "Elmer's in the hutch behind the house. I just saw him!"

"Child, you must have been imagining things," said Mrs. Johnson in a sympathetic tone of voice. "Our dear little Elmer is gone."

"No!" I screamed, refusing to listen to any more of what I perceived were lies. I broke away from my mother's embrace and took off running, bent on proving them all wrong. But when I returned to the rabbit hutch in the barn, there was no sign of Elmer and I began to cry.

Before we left the farm that day, Mrs. Johnson took my parents and me to the spot in a wilted flower garden where the rabbit had been buried. I laid a cross made from twigs on top of his grave and said good-bye to my little fluffy friend, heartbroken that I would never see him again.

I know I didn't imagine seeing Elmer in his hutch that day. And more than fifty years later, I still believe very firmly that it was his spirit that appeared to me. Perhaps that was his way of saying a final farewell to a little girl who loved him dearly.

Igor, the Supernatural Bat

by Gerina Dunwich

One of the strangest experiences I've ever had with the supernatural was a phantom bat that haunted my old Victorian house in upstate New York. Every time it visited us it would first appear in the music room before flying up the stairs to the second floor, where it would disappear into thin air.

I could never figure out how it got in or out of the house when all the doors and windows were shut tight, the front of the fireplace was sealed off to accommodate a wood-burning stove, and there were no holes or cracks in any of the walls.

The bat's mysterious visitations, which always took place in the evening hours, became so regular that I affectionately began calling it Igor, after the pet bat on the old television show *The Munsters*.

I know for a fact that Igor was not a figment of my imagination because other people (including my mother, my husband, and our friend Lisa) also saw him. At that time we had two indoor calico cats (Endora and Isadora), and whenever the bat showed up, they got very excited and would chase after it. It was amusing watching them leap into the air in their vain attempt to catch the bat as it would fly through the house.

One night when Igor paid us a visit, my husband managed to trap the bat in a paper bag, or at least so he thought. He quickly folded the top of the bag over and stapled it shut. He then put the bag in the car and drove out of town about fifteen miles to a rural area that seemed a good spot to release the bat. He could hear and feel the bat fluttering around inside the bag as he picked it up and carried it to the side of the road. But, when he opened the top of the bag to set the bat free, nothing flew out. He peeked inside the bag and discovered it was empty. He was quite puzzled, as there were no holes in the bag and no way the bat could have gotten out without him seeing it.

It didn't take long before we started seeing Igor flying through the house again. I think that's when we realized that the bat was some sort of ghost.

After the "ice storm of the century" hit in 1998 and caused

widespread damage, we sold the house and moved back to California. With new owners at the helm, the house was converted into a group home for developmentally disabled persons.

Recently, I was contacted by one of the staff members who work there. She told me that, after purchasing my old house and witnessing a number of disturbing supernatural events there, the new owners called in a Native American shaman to perform a special cleansing ritual in the hopes of putting the spirits to rest. During the ritual, the glass door on the kitchen oven shattered. She said staff and residents alike have experienced strange sounds, apparitions (including one of a ghostly cat), unexplained balls of light rolling around on the floor, and the playing of the antique piano (which I sold with the house) when no one was in the room.

I asked about the phantom bat and was told that it still appears inside the house from time to time, flies up the stairs to the second floor, and disappears without a trace.

The Owl of Death

by J. C. Blanchard

It was a snowy November night back in 1977 when the owl first appeared on my grandparents' farm in northern Maine. My grandfather, who had gone into the barn to retrieve the kerosene for a lantern, spotted something out of the corner of his eye. He turned his head to look and saw a huge owl perched on a beam. But as soon as he focused his eyes on the bird, it seemed to de-materialize.

My grandfather thought the owl must have been a figment of his imagination, and he went about his business. But on the way back to the house with the kerosene, he heard a sound like "hoo, hoo" coming from one of the trees near the garden. He looked up and saw the same owl he had seen earlier in the barn. From its branch it looked down with glowing yellow eyes and made eye contact with him. After a few seconds passed, the owl once again disappeared.

After my grandfather told this strange story to my grandmother, she got worried and told him she felt the owl was a bad omen. He laughed and told her not to be so superstitious. Three days before Thanksgiving he suffered a massive stroke and died.

Everyone in the family tried to convince my grandmother that the owl and her husband's death were just coincidental events, but she refused to accept them as such.

Two years passed and then one morning my mother received a strange phone call from my grandmother. She said she was calling to say good-bye to everyone because she would soon be joining her husband on the other side. My mother got upset and asked her what was wrong with her health. She replied that her health was okay, but she had heard the owl hooting outside her window the night before and when she raised the shade and gazed upon the creature, it faded away like mist. That's how she knew her death would be coming soon.

My mother was not a believer in omens or the supernatural, or perhaps she was secretly afraid to believe in that kind of stuff. She got mad and told her mother that she was talking utter nonsense and to stop it. She then changed the subject, talking about the weather and current events for a while, and then said good-bye and hung up the phone.

The following day I came home from school and found my mother sitting at the kitchen table with my Aunt Marie, who had driven up from Bangor. They both were teary-eyed and solemn. I immediately knew something was wrong. My mother gave me a hug and told me the news that my grandma had passed away in her sleep—just as the ghostly owl had portended.

Tea Time

by Carole Emms

The oddest thing happened to me one time when I was baby-sitting at a neighbor's house. (And, even now, just thinking about it gives me some serious chills!)

After putting the baby to bed that evening I sat down on the living room couch and started reading a book to help pass away the time. The house was very still except for the steady *tick, tick, tick* coming from the clock that sat on the fireplace mantel.

All of a sudden a voice came from the dining room and startled me. It was a strange-sounding voice, neither male nor female, and it said something that sounded like "Tea time."

I put down my book and called out, "Hello?"

I waited a minute or two but no reply came. Nervously, I tip-toed into the dining room to investigate. No one was there and nothing seemed out of place. I checked on the baby, who was fast asleep, and then returned to the living room couch where my book awaited.

I had just finished reading the first chapter when again I heard the same voice come from the dining room.

"Tea time. . . . Tea time."

My heart started to beat faster and I sat there frozen with fear, contemplating whether or not I should take the baby and flee from the house. As clips from teenage slasher movies played over and over in my head, I nervously whispered to myself, "This is just too weird."

I sat there for what felt like an eternity, waiting for the voice or the sound of approaching footsteps (in which case I know I would have run out of the house without hesitation!), but the only thing I heard was the ticking of the clock.

The baby began to cry, and the first thought that went through my mind was that someone (or something) was in her room trying to harm her. Without thinking of my own safety, I instinctively picked up the fireplace poker and charged into the baby's bedroom, ready to confront whatever threatening menace might be in there. With my adrenaline pumping violently, I switched on the light and quickly scanned the room. I was surprised (and relieved) to find no one but the baby in there. I quickly locked the bedroom door and stayed in the room with the baby until her parents returned home later that evening.

I told them about the strange voice in the dining room and the mother clearly had a shocked expression on her face. She looked at her husband and then gazed toward the dining room and said, almost to herself, "Well isn't that the queerest thing?" She then told me that her mother, whom she inherited the house from, used to have a very talkative pet mynah bird that she kept in a large cage in the dining room. Every afternoon her mother used to ask the bird what time it was, and it always replied, "Tea time."

CONTRIBUTOR BIOGRAPHIES

Linda J. Adams is a forty-four-year-old single mom and full-time Realtor. She enjoys absorbing information on all paranormal activity and unexplained phenomena through TV, movies, books, articles, lectures, the Web, and just plain conversation. She is into "ghosts, spirits, UFOs, aliens, crop circles, the Loch Ness monster, the Jersey devil, and any of life's mysteries." She also likes socializing with friends and family, writing, photography, music, and dancing.

Vikki Anderson is a metaphysics teacher, lecturer, and writer who practices and lives in northern New Jersey. For more information, please visit her website at www.VikkiAnderson.com.

Erik Bratlien (pronounced "brat-lynn") lives in Missoula, Montana. He and his son are the founders of the paranormal investigation group, Tortured Souls Investigations (T.S.I.).

Tamara Buchfelder is currently a stay-at-home mom to two wonderful children, a cat and a husband, and once upon a time had a career in the medical field. She's also done some freelance writing in the past, as well as performed in the musical theater. She says, "I haven't had another dog in my life since Sandy. . . . She's a tough act to follow."

Gerina Dunwich (see About the Author, page 198)

James Griffiths is a psychic medium, clairvoyant, and spiritual healer who has had psychic experiences since he was ten years old. In the past four years James has branched out into providing readings and workshops for spiritual awareness as well as being the "online psychic" for one of the United Kingdom's largest regional newspaper groups. Griffiths is also a Reiki master and uses his gift to heal animals and people. He is based in Cheshire, England. For more information, please visit his website at www.semajames. co.uk.

E. G. Gruebner is a retired social studies teacher who resides in Norwalk, Connecticut.

Brandy Hoffstedder is a graphic arts designer, a freelance writer, and an animal rights activist. She teaches art and yoga classes in New York, where she resides with her husband, two daughters, a Great Dane, three noisy parakeets, and an overly pampered Himalayan cat.

Sheila Hrabal has been writing since she was a child. She began her writing career by editing the Entertainment section of her high school newspaper, *The Tiger Rag*. She has a teaching degree, an associate's degree in Applied Arts and Sciences, and a bachelor's degree in Fine Arts in Visual Art Studies. Since graduating college, she has been writing articles about travel, home improvement tips, sleep apnea, alcohol abuse and treatment, horoscopes, and craft tips sheets for several websites. Her poetry has been published by the International Society of Poetry and on Poetry.com since 2000. Additionally, she has written technical manuals for CompoGraphics and Verizon and has also been a freelance fiction writer for more than twenty-five years. She has published recipes for local fund-raising cookbooks and recently completed an IRS tax deduction eBook for small business owners. Currently, Sheila is working with students to improve their grade-level comprehension as an online tutor. She resides in Irving, Texas.

Suzy Johnson is the founder of the Garrs Lane Project (an on-going haunted house investigation). She and her family reside in Louisville, Kentucky.

Amy Lynwander and **Melissa Rowell** are the owners of Fell's Point Ghost Tours, an award-winning walking ghost tour of historic Fell's Point in Baltimore, Maryland. Lynwander is originally from New Jersey. She graduated from Lehigh University in Bethlehem, Pennsylvania, and lives with her family in Fell's Point. Rowell is originally from Georgia. She graduated from West Georgia College in Carrolton, Georgia, and the Medical College of Georgia in Augusta. She lives with her family in Baltimore County. Their first book, *Baltimore's Harbor Haunts: True Ghost Stories*, was published in June of 2005. Fell's Point Ghost Tours: P.O. Box 38140, Baltimore, MD, 21231. Fore more information, please visit their website at: www.fellspointghost.com.

Ray "Eyramon" Murton is a shadowy figure, a hermit living near Round Mountain on the northern tablelands of NSW,

Australia. He lives with his dogs, horses, and various other creatures, mainly wild, which visit when inclined. The local aboriginals call him "Spirit Man" as his occult heritage parallels their "Dreamtime." He is a practicing magus/medicine man/witch of a hereditary eclectic tradition and has been, for seventy-three of his seventy-five years—having been initiated by his mother. He has "the Sight," is a healer, and is recognized as an elder of the Australian pagan community. Eyramon is available for consultations, teaching, Reiki, and numerological readings. For more information, e-mail: raymurton@yahoo.com.au or write to Kangaroo Creek Crossing, RMB 172 Guyra Road, Guy Fawkes via Ebor 2453 NSW, Australia.

Lee Prosser was born in Missouri on December 31, 1944. He has a Ph.D. in Ancient Religions and has a lifelong interest in Vedanta, Wicca, Witchcraft, and Shamanism. He is an Adept of the Order of the Golden Dawn and a Druid Adept of the Ancient Order of Druids in America. He is the author of numerous publications including the memoir *Isherwood, Bowles, Vedanta, Wicca, and Me.* His writings have appeared in *The Encyclopedia of Haunted Places* by Jeff Belanger, and the books *Dunwich's Guide to Gemstone Sorcery, A Witch's Guide to Ghosts and the Supernatural,* and *Herbal Magick* (all by Gerina Dunwich). He is the book review editor and contributor to both Ghostvillage.com and Jazzreview.com. His articles and essays include "Raymond Buckland," "The Ghost of Aldous Huxley," "India and the Supernatural," "The Golden Dawn," and "Arthur Edward Waite," among others. Prosser and his wife live in Missouri.

Russell Roberts lives in a small village north of Utica, New York, and currently works in a local hospital. His interests include fishing and hiking in the Adirondacks region, history, architecture, archaeology, bird watching, and photography.

Doris "Dusty" Smith is the president and founder of both the Daytona Beach Paranormal Research Group, Inc. (www.dbprginc. org) and the International Association of Cemetery Preservationists, Inc. She is a proud member of the TAPS (The Atlantic Paranormal Society) family and the American Ghost Society (AGS). She also owns and operates the Haunts of the World's Most Famous Beach Ghost Tours.

Eileen Smith is a holistic arts practitioner and artist. Originally from Point Pleasant, New Jersey, she now lives in Matawan, New Jersey.

Suzanne Smith is a floral artist. She lives in Huntington Beach, California. For more information, please visit her website at: suzannemsmithdesigns.com.

Athena Sydney was born and raised in the Netherlands. At the age of eighteen she moved to Switzerland and subsequently lived in half a dozen countries worldwide. Now she is back in the Netherlands and lives with her two cats in a village not too far from the North Sea. She writes fantasy, fiction, and articles on various subjects from witchcraft to current affairs. She is also the author of the fantasy novels *Heiress to Evil* and *Bracelets: Star's Quest for Avalon*. For more information, please visit her website at athena. gemstonedeva.com.

Rosemarie V. was born in La Palma, Michoacan, Mexico, and has had many experiences with the paranormal since she was a little girl. She currently lives in Fresno, California.

Michael John Weaver is the director of the San Antonio Parapsychological Association (Texas). He holds an M.S. degree in Psychology: Marriage and Family Therapy Concentration. He was born under the sign of Taurus. For more information, please visit his website at sapa.freeservers.com.

Samantha Williams lives in Oakridge, Tennessee, in a house built during World War II. Contrary to popular belief, she wasn't named after the *Bewitched* character, though her mother did watch the show. A practicing witch since the age of sixteen, she shares her life with four beautiful felines: Silver, Bastet, Sheba, and Queen Mab, and a loving companion, Seamus. Her hobbies are books (she has about a thousand), herbs, candles, watching scary movies, the tarot, and researching the history of the Craft.

BIBLIOGRAPHY

Guiley, Rosemary Ellen. *The Encyclopedia of Ghosts and Spirits*. New York: Facts on File, 1992.

———. *Harper's Encyclopedia of Mystical and Paranormal Experience*. New York: HarperCollins, 1991.

Hapgood, Sarah. *500 British Ghosts and Hauntings*. London: Foulsham, 1993.

Myers, Arthur. *Ghostly American Places* (originally titled *The Ghostly Gazetteer*). Avenel, NJ: Wings Books—a division of Random House Value Publishing, Inc., 1995.

RESOURCES

The Atlantic Paranormal Society (T.A.P.S.)
3297 Post Road
Warwick, Rhode Island 02886
E-mail: help@the-atlantic-paranormal-society.com
Website: the-atlantic-paranormal-society.com

Daytona Beach Paranormal Research Group, Inc.
E-mail: dbprgcontact@aol.com
Website: www.dbprginc.org

Fell's Point Ghost Tours
P.O. Box 38140
Baltimore, Maryland 21231
Website: www.fellspointghost.com

Garrs Lane Project
E-mail: GARRSLANEPROJECT@aol.com
Website: www.angelfire.com/weird2/scaredky

GhostVillage.com

E-mail: info@ghostvillage.com

Website: www.ghostvillage.com

Haunts of the World's Most Famous Beach Ghost Tours

Website: www.hauntsofdaytona.com

Hermetic Magick

Website: www.hermeticmagick.com

Iowa Ghost Hunters

Dallas Country, Iowa

E-mail: iaghosthunters@yahoo.com

Website: groups.yahoo.com/group/iaghosthunters

Panpipes Magickal Marketplace

1641 Cahuenga Boulevard

Hollywood, California 90028

Phone: (323) 462-7078

Website: www.panpipes.com

Paranormal Animal Research Group (PAR-Group)

c/o Gerina Dunwich

P.O. Box 4263

Chatsworth, California 91313

E-mail: gerinadunwich@yahoo.com

Website: groups.yahoo.com/group/PAR-Group

Paranormal Pugs Page

Website: starkimages.homestead.com/paranormalpugspage.html

San Antonio Parapsychological Association
P.O. Box 201203
San Antonio, Texas 78220
E-mail: psiexploration@yahoo.com
Website: sapa.freeservers.com

INDEX

ABOUT THE AUTHOR

Gerina Dunwich is a paranormal researcher and ghost hunter who specializes in animal spirits and animal-related hauntings. In October of 2005 she founded the Paranormal Animal Research Group, which focuses on the phenomenon of ghost-animals and animal psychic sensitivity to the paranormal. Dunwich is an ordained minister and a member of the International Ghost Hunters Society (IGHS) and the Author's Guild. She is also a gifted spiritualist-medium and the author of over two dozen books on witchcraft and various occult subjects. She currently lives in northwestern Pennsylvania, in a haunted nineteenth-century Victorian house.

She can be reached by e-mail at gerinadunwich@yahoo.com. Her official website is www.freewebs.com/gerinadunwich.